Rabbi
vs.
Chaplain

DVD of this debate produced by Rabbi Tovia Singer. ©2007. Used with permissed.

Unless otherwise specified, all Scriptures used by John McTernan are taken from the King James Version of the Holy Bible.

RABBI VS. CHAPLAIN
© 2007 by John McTernan

Printed in the United States of America

ISBN 1-933641-27-4

Rabbi vs. Chaplain

Is Jesus of Nazareth the Promised Jewish Messiah?

John McTernan

Contents

Additional Books By John McTernan

As America Has Done To Israel
God's Final Warning to America
Israel: The Blessing or the Curse
Father Forgive Them

Only Jesus of Nazareth Series:

Only Jesus of Nazareth
Can be Israel's King Messiah

Only Jesus of Nazareth
Can Be the God of Israel's Righteous Servant

Only Jesus of Nazareth
Can Sit On The Throne of David

John McTernan may be reached by e-mail at:
john316@defendproclaimthefaith.org

or visit his website at:
www.defendproclaimthefaith.org
www.internationalcopsforchrist.com

write:
John McTernan
P.O. Box 444,
Liverpool, PA 17045

Foreword

This book is a transcript of perhaps the most unusual debate that has ever occurred. Unusual and unimaginable from the position that the potentate of apologetic Judaism would dare to condescend to discuss, debate, or even communicate with a Christian on the theological consideration that Jesus Christ is not only Lord of Lords but the promised Messiah of Israel has heretofore been unthinkable. Even so, that the chief apologist for Judaism would even appear on the same platform with a non–kosher gentile is a doctrinal breakthrough.

In the Arab nations of North Africa, the Middle East, Indonesia, Malaysia, and wherever Islam pervades, Mohammed is venerated and worshipped as a great prophet of Allah. In India, China, and the other nations of Southeast Asia, there are countless temples and idols in recognition of the spiritual teachings of Buddha. Yet, in the historical records of Israel, museums and public buildings, streets and monuments, there is no hint of the life or teachings of the greatest Jew who ever lived. This same Jew—Jesus Christ—who has been the cultural and spiritual foundation of the Western world, and believed on as the very Son of God by conception, who is believed on and worshipped by one–third of the earth's population, is still considered as nothing more than a rabble–rouser who was condemned to death by a Roman prelate as the insistence of the Sanhedrin.

Rabbi Tovia Singer in this debate presents the standard argument of Judaic orthodoxy that the prophecies in the Old Testament, even including Isaiah 53, could not possibly refer to Jesus Christ, because Jesus did not fulfill the messianic promises concerning Israel. Yet, as we and others have pointed out, in Jeremiah alone, eight times the prophet said that Israel would not know the time of their visitation, and in many other prophetic passages, the breach that would occur between God and Israel is foretold, and even His death, resurrection, and second coming is clearly declared (Dan. 9:26; Hosea 5:15; 6:1–3, etc.).

Regardless of the issues discussed in this debate concerning Jesus Christ as Israel's Messiah, evangelical Christians like John McTernan and myself are the best friends that Israel has in the world today. We love the Jews because God loves them (Rom. 10:1; 11:1–2). Christians reading this transcript and watching the accompanying DVD can better understand why Jews still today reject Jesus Christ as their Messiah; and Jews likewise can better understand why Christians the world over believe that He is the Lord of Lords, King of Kings, the Blessed Saviour forever of all who place their faith in Him.

—N. W. Hutchings

Introduction

The following is the transcript of a debate that took place on February 19, 2006, at the Bukhariah Jewish Center, Forest Hills, New York. Rabbi Tovia Singer represented Judaism while Chaplain John McTernan of International Cops for Christ represented Christianity.

Rabbi Singer is specially trained as a counter–missionary to thwart the gospel of Jesus Christ. He travels all over the United States and the world to teach Jews how to refute Christian doctrines. He is one of the leading counter–missionaries in the world. His website and teaching series are aimed at refuting the gospel.

Chaplain McTernan has spent thousands of hours with Judaism's counter–missionaries in defending the gospel of Jesus Christ. This resulted in him obtaining unique knowledge in how to defend and proclaim the gospel from the Old Testament. Chaplain McTernan used this fine–honed knowledge during this debate.

The debate was actually two sessions that took place consecutively, plus a question–and–answer period. The topic of the first debate was *"Is Jesus the Promised Jewish Messiah?"* The second topic was *"Without the Shedding of Blood There Is No Atonement."* This debate was before an entirely Jewish audience. Because Jews do not accept the New Testament as the Word of God, Chaplain McTernan stayed primarily within the Old Testament during both debates. The Old Testament is the foundation for the New Testament. The debate brings out these foundations and shows the truth that Jesus of Nazareth is Israel's Messiah.

During this debate on a few occasions, the voice of Rabbi Singer is low and difficult to understand. Please use this transcript to aid you during these occasions. On a few occasions, the rabbi used Hebrew words which were not translated. The voice of Chaplain McTernan is understandable at all times.

The debate was transcribed because it is an excellent teaching tool. The text gives you the ability to study what is being taught and how the teachings of the New Testament have a solid foundation in the Old Testament. It is recommended that you listen to the debate a few times to get the full impact of the scriptures that were used. The post–debate part of this book involves Chaplain McTernan's expansion of the information developed during the debate.

Chaplain McTernan has authored three books proving that Jesus of Nazareth is Israel's Messiah. All of his books were written based on this interaction with Judaism's counter–missionaries. The books present unique and conclusive ways to prove that Jesus of Nazareth is Israel's Messiah. Chaplain McTernan drew upon this information during the debate.

These books are:

Only Jesus of Nazareth Can Be Israel's King Messiah
Only Jesus of Nazareth Can Sit On The Throne of David
Only Jesus of Nazareth Can Be The God Of Israel's Righteous Servant

The debate gives a foundation, and Chaplain McTernan's books provide additional scriptures and concepts which build upon this foundation.

Chapter One

The First Debate:
Is Jesus the Promised Jewish Messiah

The general opening remarks by the moderator were not transcribed, along with the rabbi's opening prayer.

Introduction by Moderator to the debate

My name is Shalom Lamb and I'll be serving as the moderator for the debate. Both of our debaters have received written rules of the debate and timing of the debate and we will review that together in just a minute. I would like to reiterate what the rabbi said so beautifully.

We are gathered today as friends, and although we will disagree very profoundly on profoundly important issues, we are gathered as friends.

The most difficult part of the debate is now, when I request again that everyone kindly turn off the telephones. Once it is done I would like to relate to you just one observation that my wife Tina had on the way here this morning. About six hundred fifty years ago, the Rambam Maimonides entered into such a debate in Barcelona, Spain. And, as a result of that debate he was forced to flee from his home, and to leave Spain and never return again. We are tremendously blessed to live in this country, and we are blessed to live at this time. I think it is appropriate to acknowledge how fortunate we are to have this debate, and to have it as free people in a free country.

And now to the task at hand. It is my pleasure to introduce to you

Mr. John McTernan.

We have all done terrible things with your name. We are trying to get it right.

Mr. McTernan is the founder of the Branch of David Ministries, and has spent thousands of hours debating with Jews and Muslims and corresponding in defense of the gospel. During numerous appearances on television, radio, and seminars he has publicly defended Israel in light of biblical prophecy. Mr. McTernan is a true lover of Israel. Since 1975 he has been involved in the pro–life movement, and is currently a pro–life leader in Central Pennsylvania. In the early 1980s he cofounded International Cops for Christ, where he serves as an ordained chaplain and an evangelist. John holds a B.S. from Virginia Commonwealth University in Richmond, Virginia. He served for twenty–six years as a federal treasury agent before retiring in 1998. He is the author of *God's Final Warning to America* and *Father Forgive Them,* and coauthor of the best–seller *Israel: The Blessing or the Curse,* and the King Messiah series, titles: *Jesus of Nazareth: King Messiah,* and *King Messiah in His Holy Temple.* He has written several tracts including *Mohammad or Jesus the Prophet Like Unto Moses.*

Our other debater is Rabbi Tovia Singer. Tovia Singer is the host of one of Israel's most compelling radio talk show hosts. And the director of the counter–cult organization Outreach Judaism. I personally have heard Rabbi Singer speak and debate many, many places across the country like Nacogdoches, Texas, and other unpronounceable names. The Tovia Singer Show, which was launched back in January 2002 in New York, has become a powerful and provocative voice of reason in radio on Israel National Radio and in the United States. The live program is driven by compelling insights and dynamitic insights and dynamic style of its renowned host Rabbi Tovia Singer. Previous newsmaker guests on the Tovia Singer Show include Ambassador Jean Kirkpatrick, Allen Keys, Professor Allen Dershowitz, and the well–known Daniel Pipes.

Rabbi Tovia Singer is well–known as the founder and director of

Outreach Judaism, an international organization dedicated to countering the efforts of fundamentalist group and cults who specifically target Jews for conversion. As a world renowned public speaker, Rabbi Singer addresses more than two hundred audiences a year. Rabbi Singer has been an inspiration to thousands. Lecturing in college campuses and synagogues all over the country has become an integral part of his work. He is the author of the book and accompanying audiotape series titled *Let's Get Biblical*. He is a frequent guest on television and radio shows. And I recommend to everyone who's not heard the tape series, it is extraordinary and very, very worthwhile.

Finally, here is how our format will work today. There will actually be two debates and then one question–and–answer period. I would ask you to please hold your questions for the question–and–answer period. The way the debates will work are as a college debate would work. There is a resolve, which means there is a statement. The first statement will be resolved: *Jesus Is the Promised Jewish Messiah* is the affirmative action that John will take. Mr. McTernan will open with his opening statement, will be responded by Tovia Singer, then Mr. McTernan, Tovia Singer, one more time. And then each will have a two minute closing statement.

The second debate will be resolved: *Without the Shedding of Blood There is No Atonement*.

Obviously, again, that is Mr. McTernan's affirmative statement. He will open again with an eight–minute presentation and an eight–minute response by Rabbi Singer. And then two series of three–minute responses and then a closing statement.

That will be end of the second debate. After which will be a question–and–answer period, and—having been through a few of them before—things can get fairly lively.

So, without further ado, it is my pleasure to introduce John McTernan, who will be on this side, and Tovia Singer who will be.

First Debate:

Is Jesus the Promised Jewish Messiah

Part One

Chaplain John McTernan

I feel like I am back in college. Thank you for having me. Thank you Tovia.

In the time I have in opening, to answer the argument that was put forward, I was thinking, what is the very foundation of my faith?

The very foundation of my faith is that Jesus of Nazareth is the God of Israel. That's the very foundation of the Christian faith.

And, when I look at scriptures, I want to give you two series of scriptures, and put them together in the time we have. The key to it in my opinion would be found in the prophet Zechariah, starting in chapter six. If you have your Bibles you can turn with me to it.

And starting in chapter 6, verse 9, we have the word of the Lord to the prophet Zechariah. That he is to take gold and silver from them returning from Babylon, and he's to put crowns on the head of Joshua, who was the high priest at that time. And I'd like to read those Scriptures. We come to Zechariah 6:11:

> Then take silver and gold, and make crowns, and set them
> upon the head of Joshua the son of Josedech, the high priest;
> And speak unto him, saying, Thus speaketh the LORD of

hosts, saying, Behold the man whose name is The BRANCH.
—Zechariah 6:11–12

So in this verse we have the prophet Zechariah speaking to one person, who at that time was the high priest of Israel, Joshua.

I always tell people—and I know I probably don't have to do it here—he is not confused with Joshua at the time of Moses. This is Joshua at the time of the Babylonian captivity. And he says to put crowns on his head. But he addresses the high priest as the Branch, which I'll shortly explain. And he says:

Behold the man whose name is The BRANCH; and he shall grow up out of his place, and he shall build the temple of the LORD: Even he shall build the temple of the LORD; and he shall bear the glory, and shall sit and rule upon his throne; and he shall be a priest upon his throne: and the counsel of peace shall be between them both.
—Zechariah 6:12–13

When you study the word *Branch*—and that is how it is translated into English, and I understand there are various words in Hebrew it can be translated into—but when you study that word through the Scripture, the *Branch* is a terminology that is set for the Messiah.

You can see this in Jeremiah 23:4–5. I want to read this very quickly, Jeremiah 23:

Behold, the days come, saith the LORD, that I will raise unto David a righteous Branch, and a King shall reign and prosper, and shall execute judgment and justice in the earth. In his days Judah shall be saved, and Israel shall dwell safely: and this is his name whereby he shall be called, THE LORD OUR RIGHTEOUSNESS.
—Jeremiah 23:5–6

So, we have the Messiah, the Son of David referred to as the Branch.

But here in Zechariah, we have the high priest of Israel, also being referred to as the Branch. And notice what it says here: that this particular person, the Branch, He is going to build the temple of the Lord, and He shall bear the glory, and He shall sit upon and rule upon His throne.

This has to be the throne of David.

It can only be the throne of David.

The Messiah does not sit on any throne but the throne of David. And it says, He shall bear the glory, which the Branch is going to do.

Notice this, he shall be a priest upon His throne. When I study the Word of God and I look into the Torah, priests don't sit on thrones. Priests don't wear crowns. The high priest of Israel wears a mitre around his head, with a band in front, which says "Holiness Unto the LORD." It is impossible according to the law of Moses, for one person to be the high priest of Israel and to be the king, the Son of David because of the genealogy. You are either from the line of David or from the line of Aaron. The two can never meet.

And it says the counsel of peace shall be between them both. Notice He shall sit and rule upon this throne.

Now when we go to the Scriptures, and we see the Messiah sitting on His throne—it all comes together, my belief that the Messiah is the God of Israel.

We see this in Ezekiel 43, when we have the messianic era, the messianic temple, the Messiah builds the temple. We come to Ezekiel 43, and this is what the prophet Ezekiel says:

> **Afterward he brought me to the gate, even the gate that looketh toward the east: And, behold, the glory of the God of Israel came from the way of the east: and his voice was like a noise of many waters: and the earth shined with his glory.**
>
> —Ezekiel 43:1–2

So here the prophet sees the holy God of Israel. And he sees the temple, the messianic temple.

> **And the glory of the LORD came into the house by the way of the gate whose prospect is toward the east.**
>
> —Ezekiel 43:4

So that the prophet sees the glory of the God of Israel, coming through the East Gate, and coming into the Messiah's temple. Remember according to Zechariah, the Messiah is going to build the temple of the LORD, and sit on the throne of David.

> **So the spirit took me up, and brought me into the inner court; and, behold, the glory of the LORD filled the house.**
>
> —Ezekiel 43:5

So Ezekiel had been on the outer court, the temple of the LORD is going to have a large outer court. And then it's going to have a smaller inner court. And there's gates on these courts. There is an outer gate and then an inner gate. Then there's the temple that's inside the inner court. I wish I had more time explain that but I don't.

> **So the spirit took me up, and brought me into the inner court.**

So Ezekiel the prophet is now inside the inner court. And he's looking into the temple. The temple that the Messiah is going to build. He's right there, looking in, and this is what he sees:

> **So the spirit took me up, and brought me into the inner court; and, behold, the glory of the LORD filled the house. And I heard him speaking unto me out of the house.**
>
> —Ezekiel 43:5–6

He heard the God of Israel speaking to him. And this is what the God of Israel says:

> **And he said unto me, Son of man, the place of my throne, and the place of the soles of my feet, where I will dwell in the midst of the children of Israel for ever, and my holy name, shall the house of Israel no more defile, neither they, nor their kings. . . .**
>
> —Ezekiel 43:7

It goes on but that is fine enough.

What we have here is when Ezekiel looks into the Messiah's temple, and he looks at the throne that's in the Messiah's temple, who is sitting on it but the God of Israel in His glory. According the prophet Zechariah, this should be the Messiah sitting on the throne of David. But when Ezekiel sees, when Ezekiel sees the temple, and he looks in, it's the holy God of Israel in His glory, sitting on the throne. And we can see that this is literal, because we go to Ezekiel 44. There is no reason not to take this literal. Ezekiel 44:1:

> **Then he brought me back the way of the gate of the outward sanctuary which looketh toward the east; and it was shut. Then said the LORD unto me; This gate shall be shut, it shall not be opened, and no man shall enter in by it; because the LORD, the God of Israel, hath entered in by it.**
>
> —Ezekiel 44:1–2

So who has entered into the gate?

Why is the gate shut?

Because the holy God of Israel in His glory entered in through it. The gate is going to be permanently shut. Ezekiel saw the glory go into the inner court. Ezekiel saw the glory go into the temple. Ezekiel looked in and he heard the LORD's voice, and it was the holy God of

Israel sitting on the throne of David.

And as a Christian, that's exactly what I believe, that the holy God of Israel is none other than Jesus of Nazareth. Of course there is a lot more I could develop on that, but I think that . . .

(Do I have a minute left. . . okay, I knew I was getting close)

If you go to the very end of Ezekiel, if you go to the last chapter in Ezekiel and the last verse, this is what it says. In Ezekiel, I think your Bible lines up with mine as far as numbering. Ezekiel 48:35, says:

> **. . . and the name of the city from that day shall be, The LORD is there.**

So the holy God of Israel is literally in Israel, in Jerusalem. He is literally in the temple. And, I believe, He is in the Holy of Holies, sitting on the throne of David, and that's the throne, and that's the location where the Messiah of Israel will sit.

So the Messiah of Israel and the holy God of Israel, are one in the same. And that is very heart of my faith.

Rabbi Tovia Singer

I want to begin this afternoon's presentation by first of all stating that, John, I'm an orthodox rabbi.

And we believe that the Bible is the Word of God.

We trust the Scriptures alone.

We don't trust Tony Blair.

We don't trust the Quartet.

We don't trust Putin.

We trust *Tanakh* [Old Testament], we trust our Bible.

And that alone is my authority; I have no other.

And it is from this Bible we will seek today.

The Messiah is to bring about a world where there would be security for Judah. That is what you just heard. Scripture tells us as we have been quoted, the messianic age will bring about a temple, that will stand in Jerusalem.

This is true, in fact the book of Ezekiel, the same scripture you just heard, the last verse you just heard, the last verse in chapter 37, tells us when that temple stands in Jerusalem, than the gentiles—that's you, the *Goyhim*—they will know that I am LORD.

Now we have to ask ourselves the question, look you know that I have an opinion. We as Jews, we are opinionated people. And Christians, you all have your opinions. But then ask yourself a question, what is God's opinion?

I don't know how many years I have left.

We are living in extraordinary time.

What does God think about all this?

That's where we are after today.

The temple would be built, the Scripture says. In fact, the last nine chapters of Ezekiel as we heard here, describes vividly, what that temple will look like.

Scripture tells that when Messiah comes, there will be peace that will reign throughout the world. Nation will not lift up sword against another nation. Neither will they learn of war any more.

The Bible says that the messianic age will be an ingathering of the exiles—the north, the south, give forth my children.

Scriptures teaches us that in the messianic age, as you heard, the knowledge of God will cover the world as the water covers the sea (Isaiah 11).

[*Rabbi sings in Hebrew and cannot be translated*]

What do you think that is a signal to fold up your *talus*?

In those days the whole world will know about the one God of Abraham, Isaac and Jacob. And the dead will arise—Daniel 12:2; Isaiah 26:19; Ezekiel 37, the same book we heard before.

Now we have to ask ourselves this question, the advent of Jesus brought about safety in Judah that you speak of? Did the advent of Christianity when Jesus roamed this world, did it bring about building of the temple in Jerusalem?

What does the Bible say? What does the Scriptures say?

In the clearest terms, does the Bible, does our *Tanakh*, does those holy Scriptures teach that when Messiah comes, there would be a world going on when it is not absolutely.

What happened in the days of Jesus? I mean, we as Jews have to ask ourselves a question: was there a temple built in the first century? I mean, what you are saying is Jesus will sit on the throne of God, as described in Ezekiel 40–48.

Was there a temple built in that first century? Oh no, in the year A.D. 70, that horrible time, the temple was destroyed.

Is that your idea of a Messiah?

During the first century was there peace on earth, as described by the book of Isaiah?

[*Rabbi speaking in Hebrew*]

And the lamb will lay with the lion—Isaiah 11. Oh no, there was great war with the Romans.

During that first century was there a resurrection of the dead, as Daniel 12:2 says? Some will arise to everlasting life, others to everlasting contempt and damnation.

You see, I as a Jew, John, have to ask myself the question, who am I to trust?

And we know each other. I just want to say that we're friends.

But frankly if I have to choose between you and the God of Israel, I've got to go with Scripture; I've got to go with the Almighty.

I can't trust the cross. But I've got the book of Ezekiel, but I've got the book of Isaiah that declares the Jews will be ingathered into the land of Israel.

What happened during that first century? During that first century, Jews were not gathered into the Holy Land. And in the year 70, the Jews were exiled from the land. Was there a worldwide knowledge of God that exploded during the first century? Oh no.

As a result of that horrible exile, the Jews were thrown out the land of Israel and spread throughout the Roman Empire.

Now you're going to hear this in the come back: he is going to say to you, well there is a second coming. It didn't happen yet . . . but it will. Somehow all these wonderful prophecies will happen.

And I say to you, John, you speak about all these wonderful things, and why Jesus is the Messiah.

I will ask you . . . I could not have possibly made a better case why Jesus is incapable of being the Messiah, than the one you just made here.

All these prophecies point in one direction, and that is there have been hundreds of people throughout history, who have claimed to be the Messiah or that claim was made for them—Jesus included.

What do they all have in common? Not a single one of these prophecies have been fulfilled.

You used terms like the priest of the LORD. But, you see, the word "priest" doesn't necessarily mean a priest from Aaron. Abraham in Genesis 14 is called a priest. The Bible says that David and his children are priests.

Now how can you be from the house of David and be a priest? The word priest, the word *kohane*, this is important, because many of us don't understand this. The word *kohane* means this: it means—listen carefully—it means to hold office. It means that you are a leader. In fact, I'll say something that is going to be so strange, you'll say, "Wow, I didn't know that."

The Bible says that leaders of idolatry, those who sought to bring Baal to the Jewish people, do you know what they were called, *kohanic* Baal. They, too, are *kohanic*. Maybe the priest of Baal is going to the Messiah?

Does that make sense to anyone? The priest that we are talking about is a priest that I am. 'Cause I'm a priest; I know about my tribe, I know about my family. The priest is the person who is a son of Aaron, if you are an Aaronic priest.

Now you said this temple is going to be called God?

The Messiah is going to be called God?

This is also a problem of lexicon. It is a problem of the KJV, the King James Version.

Let me explain this point in Scripture, Again, this is going to come as a surprise to you, but we have to. That's why I said in the beginning we have to go to the Bible, because that's my authority.

Listen like you never listened in your life.

In the Bible those who represent God, or those things that represent the message of God, are called God.

How strange.

In fact, Moses, I guess he is also called a God in Exodus 7:1. The Almighty says to Moses, "You are to go to Pharaoh, and you will be a god to him. Aaron will be your prophet."

Does that mean I have to worship Moses? In Isaiah 7:10 he is called *Yod Hay Vov Hay*. He is literally called God. Does that mean Isaiah— God forbid—should be called God?

In fact the Christian Bible, and the Hebrew too, understands this issue when it refers to the Book of Psalms . . .

[*Rabbi uses Hebrew*]

You have made him a little lower then [*uses Hebrew*] the means angels.

You have to be very careful. Context is always determinative.

Now I'll say and I don't know Shalom how much time I have left. I have one minute. I will say this. You will hear about, as we have heard from every messianic type group—we have many, many organizations of religion, yours included, that has hoped and wished that their God, that their leader would be the Messiah, and they said he's coming He's the Messiah, then something irregular would occur, something disappointing would happen.

The man died and not a single prophecy was filled.

And what do you have to say then second coming.

Now I concede this point and end on this point, although a second coming does conveniently explain away any false messiah, the idea is not articulated clearly in a single scripture in the Jewish Scriptures.

This is why I am a Jew, because this Bible says to follow the God of Israel and not—God forbid—a Jesus of Nazareth.

Thank you.

Part Two

Chaplain McTernan

I agree with Tovia, Rabbi Tovia Singer about one thing, and that's the final authority is the word of God. Not me, not him, but what Moses and the prophets wrote.

And I clearly showed in my presentation, that the holy God of Israel is sitting on the Messiah's throne. That is the very foundation, the very heart of Christianity, that Messiah is the God of Israel.

Now I want to show you a couple more Scriptures. Just, I'd like to respond to one thing that Rabbi Tovia Singer said about the two comings. Let's go to Zechariah 9, and starting at verse 9:

Rejoice greatly, O daughter of Zion; shout, O daughter of Jerusalem: behold, thy King cometh unto thee: he is just, and having salvation; lowly, and riding upon an ass, and upon a colt the foal of an ass.

And the next verse says:

And I will cut off the chariot from Ephraim, and the horse from Jerusalem, and the battle bow shall be cut off: and he shall speak peace unto the heathen: and his dominion shall be from sea even to sea, and from the river even to the ends of the earth.

—Zechariah 9:10

Here are the two comings of the Messiah. The first coming He is coming lowly with salvation on a donkey. The second one, we look at the scripture in verse 10, and that is the Day of the LORD, that's when the Messiah comes and destroys the enemies of Israel. The only thing the scripture doesn't say—there is a gap between them.

We go to Daniel, the prophet Daniel, chapter 7, and here is the Messiah coming to sit on the throne of David. This is what the Bible says, ". . . and I saw in the night visions"

Excuse me Daniel 7:13:

I saw in the night visions, and, behold, one like the Son of man came with the clouds of heaven.

And I believe the "clouds of heaven" when you look in context, are all the believers that are in Heaven with the holy God of Israel. There has been a resurrection and they are returning with the Messiah. That's what the "clouds of heaven" are.

. . . and came to the Ancient of days, and they brought him near before him. And there was given him dominion, and glory, and a kingdom, that all people, nations, and languages, should serve him: his dominion is an everlasting dominion, which shall not pass away, and his kingdom that which shall not be destroyed.

—Daniel 7:13–14

At the Messiah's first coming, he came lowly on a donkey with our salvation.

It's exactly what Jesus of Nazareth did. He bought our salvation with His own blood on the cross at Calvary.

The Second Coming, He's coming with the "clouds of heaven." And He is coming to establish His kingdom.

And when He establishes His kingdom, He is going to enter in through the Eastern Gate of the temple, which He's going to build. He's going to walk through the Eastern Gate in His glory. The gate is then going to be sealed. He's going to walk through the inner gate. This is what Ezekiel saw. He is going walk to right into the temple.

And when you are at the temple of the LORD in Ezekiel, you will see there is no Menorah. There is no Table of Shew Bread. There is no Alter of Incense. There is no veil. There is no brazen laver for water for washing.

The reason is the Messiah fulfilled all of this. He is the Bread of Life. He is the Light of the world. He is the sweet savor unto the LORD. So these items are removed. The opening, there is no veil anymore, like the law of Moses requires. And He is the throne of David. The Ark of the Covenant is removed. There will be no Ark of the Covenant when the Messiah reigns.

This is what Jeremiah 3:16 says:

And it shall come to pass, when ye be multiplied and increased in the land, in those days, saith the LORD.

Now notice this:

They shall say no more, The ark of the covenant of the LORD: neither shall it come to mind: neither shall they remember it; neither shall they visit it; neither shall that be done any more. At that time they shall call Jerusalem the throne of the LORD; and all the nations shall be gathered unto it, to the name of the LORD, to Jerusalem: neither shall they walk any more after the imagination of their evil heart.

The Messiah will sit; there will be no Ark. The Ark is going to be removed. It will be replaced by the throne of David. And Jesus of Nazareth will sit on that throne in His glory.

Thank you

Rabbi Singer

What a wonderful time Jesus has brought for us. He has brought us a great temple sitting in Jerusalem, where the world sees peace. I'm so happy that we had Jesus, to bring about this extraordinary time. And I look out into the world and I wonder to myself, if there is supposed to be world peace, why is that so many are dying at the hands of Islam?

I look at the temple mount today, and I don't see, and I don't see a [Hebrew word] that was built by Jesus of Nazareth.

I see the Dome of the Rock and al Aqsa. Those are two witnesses that are bearing witness to you, John, that the Messiah has not come.

You quote from Ezekiel chapter 44 and 43 and 48. Let's see what Ezekiel describes about this temple. There won't be a law, there won't be an Ark of the Covenant, and therefore Jesus fulfilled the law for us.

Maybe we could go home and eat any food we wish. Shabbat could be set away, God forbid. And all the commandments described in that scroll could be abandoned.

What you didn't quote is Ezekiel 44:9 that says no one, no man who is either, uncircumcised of the flesh or the heart can enter that temple.

Yet, your Christianity that you worship and embrace, says that you don't need circumcision; that's over with. In fact Galatians 5:5–6 says if you are circumcised, Christ will avail you nothing. [Inaudible] of the Messiah, please God, it is on the way soon. But Ezekiel 44:9 from the same scripture you quote from says explicitly that you must have circumcision.

Wait we are not done yet. Let's keep going on in the book of Ezekiel 44. Let's go to verse 23 and 24. These are such delicious verses.

I hope when you go home you'll open up that *Tanakh* you possess, crack it open and munch like honey on your hand.

What does it say there? It says there, listen to me, that the Jewish people that they keep the commandments, and observe all the statutes. That's what it says there.

Then I go to John's pastor and ask him, you know, tell me something, do I have to keep these commandments?

Oh no, the Sabbath is done with, although those scriptures says it is forever.

If I go to the Christians and say, well, do the Jews have to keep kosher, tithe for charity, cloth the naked, care for the orphan and widow, they'll say, not really, the law is done with.

Now we have the cross.

You see, that is exactly the opposite of what Ezekiel says, as Ezekiel 37:24 which describes [*Hebrew words*] Christianity.

And in the thirty seconds I have left: Jeremiah 3:16, it describes the messianic age, that says that, it doesn't say there won't be an Ark. The people will not call upon the Ark. There will not be a need for the Ark of the Covenant.

What does that mean?

Read the context, it is always determinative. The Jewish people when we went to war, what did we put in front of the battle? The Ark of the Covenant to protect us in time of war.

In the messianic age you won't need that Ark of the Covenant in war, because there will not be war. War is with us today. When the true Messiah comes—it was not Jesus—there will not be war, but there will be peace on earth.

Thank you

Part Three

Chaplain McTernan

My object here was to prove that the Messiah is the God of Israel.

In the second section we are going to show the need for the blood, and the first coming and second coming of the Messiah—excuse me, the need for blood in the atonement for sin.

But let me, I think in this debate Jeremiah 3 is critical. Let me read you Jeremiah 3:16–17. . . and I'll read it very slowly:

And it shall come to pass, when ye be multiplied and increased in the land, in those days, saith the LORD . . .

Now that context when you read the whole section, means the messianic reign. It's not talking about when Israel is restored to the land. It's the messianic reign:

. . . in those days, saith the LORD, they shall say no more, The ark of the covenant of the LORD . . .

In the time of Moses the temple was built around the Ark. Not the Ark, it's true what the rabbi says about the Ark. The Ark was taken into battle. But, you could not have Yom Kippur without the Ark. You couldn't have it. The blood was taken and sprinkled on what we call the Mercy Seat, the top of the Ark. It was sprinkled in the front. The high priest would actually walk on the sprinkled blood into the Holy of Holies once a year.

If there is no Ark, what happened to the law of Moses? And I'm saying the law of Moses was fulfilled by the Messiah.

Now listen to this, it says here:

. . . they shall say no more, The ark of the covenant of the LORD: neither shall it come to mind . . .

How could you not think of the Ark when you read the law of Moses?

. . . neither shall they remember it . . .

They are not going to think of the Ark . . .

. . . neither shall they visit it; . . .

How can you have, how can you have the law of Moses in effect without the Ark? They're not going to think of it. They're not going to go to it. They're not going to visit it.

> **. . . neither shall that be done any more. At that time they shall call Jerusalem the throne of the LORD; and all the nations shall be gathered unto it, . . .**

There's the messianic reign. The nations are going to come to Jerusalem.

> **. . . to the name of the LORD, to Jerusalem: neither shall they walk any more after the imagination of their evil heart.**

When we go to Ezekiel 40–48, when the Messiah is reigning during the messianic era, there is no Ark of the Covenant. It has been replaced by the throne of David.

The Ark of the Covenant is a type of the throne of David. And sitting on that throne is the holy God of Israel. That is the foundation of Christianity. That the holy God of Israel is the Messiah, is the Messiah. And we believe that is Jesus of Nazareth.

Rabbi Tovia Singer

I agree the foundation of Christianity is what you just articulated.

And I will also say it is for that reason, that because of that foundation of Christianity that millions of Jews throughout history were willing to have the sword go through their neck rather than embrace this religion.

If in fact Christianity had not taught such ideas then I can assure you that many more Jews might have stumbled into this religion.

You claim that the Messiah is suppose to be God. That is a very serious charge. With worship the Messiah as though He were God, in fact your theology teaches He was God manifested in the flesh.

You know there are hundreds of prophecies about the Messiah outlined in the Jewish Scriptures, about the messianic age. Most of them are about how the world will be transformed. Very few of them are about the Messiah Himself.

There is a reason for that. He is relatively unimportant to what will happen and how the world will be transformed.

But we do have a precious few verses—and I want to make this clear—that all Christians and Jews agree, are specifically about the Messiah.

One of the most famous is Isaiah 11. The first verse describes the genealogy of Jesus, of the genealogy of the Messiah.

That was a very big mistake, excuse me—the genealogy, huge excuse me. That was the biggest excuse me in the world.

In Isaiah 11, what do we have there?

First the genealogy of the Messiah Himself; He has to come from Jesse. I say Jesus because who you claim was born from a virgin, didn't even have a human Jewish father with which to trace His genealogy back to King David.

According to you, He only had a human mother, no human father. He is therefore by the virgin birth ineligible to be the Messiah.

But in the next two verses we have something very interesting. Verse 2 and 3 tell about Him. I like to know about Him.

Maybe it says in Isaiah 11:2 that He will die on the cross—not a word about it. Maybe it says He will atone for our sins—not a word about it. It says that He will be a righteous man. A man who will not judge others after the sight of His eyes. Now listen to this [*inaudible*]. This is what Messiah is going to be like.

You hear, this is Isaiah talking, and that's what we are interested in. He says and He will fear God. I want to say that again. It says the Messiah is going to fear God. And in fact if you are not sure about that, that's stated again in verse 3. These words: "He will be quickened, filled with the fear of the LORD."

Now I ask you a question, if the Messiah is to be God, does God fear anything? Does God fear God? Is He schizophrenic? Do we need to put Him on an IV immediately? Get a drip going for Him?

The Messiah is to fear God. He is not God, that's what my Bible says.

Conclusion

Chaplain McTernan

In this debate it is very serious, because if Jesus of Nazareth is the holy God of Israel, and you reject Him, you reject the atonement which He brings. If He is not the holy God of Israel, I guess you could say idolatry.

The line is really drawn. And I think in the second debate is really going to sum the whole thing up together, because of the need of shed blood to pay for the price of sin.

And in this debate, I believe when you look at the Scriptures, like I showed you in Zechariah, and then we go over to Ezekiel, you will see the foundation of my faith is right in the Torah—excuse me—right in the *Tanakh*. It's right there, it's not manufactured, it's made, it's right out in front of you that the Messiah is going to build the temple.

Remember the prophet is speaking to the high priest of Israel, who he refers to as the Branch. And the Branch is the Son of David, who the high priest is being identified now with as the Son of David.

That is going to build the temple of the LORD. He is going to sit on His throne. He's going to act as a priest on the throne. And the counsel of peace is going to be between them both.

The Scriptures, eight chapters on the Messiah's temple, Ezekiel 40–48 (maybe that is nine chapters), and when you read that, when you read those scriptures, who is on the throne of David? The holy God of Israel.

Not only is it the holy God of Israel, but He is in His glory.

And it's literal because the temple, the Eastern Gate, is going to be shut.

So I believe I have proven the position I came here to do, that the Messiah is the holy God of Israel, who I believe is Jesus of Nazareth.

Thank you very much

Rabbi Tovia Singer

I, I, you did not address at all, the explicit Scripture in Isaiah 11 that says the Messiah will fear God.

Why would God fear Himself?

It is very clear that the Messiah is like David. In fact, He is called David by the Bible in Ezekiel 37. And David will be king, as if David. He is called David because, like David, he is a human being, not a god–man.

If you want to learn about a god–men, you go to the East; you learn about that. You go to Buddhism, Hinduism and all these [inaudible] religions. That's where you have earthly, the Zeus, not for the Jewish people. That's what's clear in Scripture.

What Zechariah 6 says is that there is going to be peace between the king and priest. Unlike—not they will be the same.

Unlike what has occurred in the past, particularly at the beginning of the second temple, and the first temple there was such tension, between the priesthood and the king, what we find in the Bible is very, very clear: that the Jewish people are to serve the one God of Israel, and no one else.

Isn't it interesting that not a single verse anywhere in the Jewish *Tanakh*, that describes the Messiah dying for our sins, and He is to be a God and a man, not one.

But the Bible says the Messiah is going to teach Torah, and as a result the Jews will keep it.

And there will be a temple sitting in Jerusalem. Right now we have two mosques that are there, filled with terror that is a testimony that the Messiah has not come.

But be strong and of good courage my brothers and sisters, because He will come, will come soon—the true Messiah. May it be quickly in our time.

Thank you

End of first debate

Chapter Two

Second Debate:
Without the Shedding of Blood There Is No Atonement

Part One

Introduction by moderator

Thus concludes the first debate. Debate two begins, resolved: *"Without the shedding of blood this is no atonement,"* which opens with John McTernan.

Chaplain McTernan

We are going to address, *Without the shedding of blood there is no atonement for sin.*

When we look at Scriptures and we go into Genesis, and we see that God created, we see that as He created day by day He said, *"It was good, it was good, it was good."* And when He created man, and He finished His creation, He says it was *"Very good."*

There is no mention of sin.

There is not mention of death.

It was very good.

We get to Genesis 3, and we see where man fell into sin. And then when we go into Genesis 4—I'm not going into four with Cain and Able—but we go into Genesis 9, and we can see for the very first time that officially recorded in the Torah the shedding of blood.

And let's go and look at this in Genesis 9—excuse me—Genesis 8:20. This is right after Noah returns after the flood, and it says:

> **And Noah builded an altar unto the LORD; and took of every clean beast, and of every clean fowl, and offered burnt offerings on the altar.**

This is the first offering made in Scriptures. Noah—notice that Noah is way before the law—Noah knew to build an altar. Scripture doesn't say how he knew. He just knew to do it.

Notice it says there was clean beasts before the law of Moses. God from the very beginning God instituted the clean and unclean.

He instituted the sacrificial system. And I believe when we look at Scriptures as a whole you will see that sacrificial system was initiated because of sin.

Now, the next verse tells you this. Okay, let me read verse 20 again:

> **And Noah builded an altar unto the LORD; and took of every clean beast, and of every clean fowl, and offered burnt offerings on the altar. And the LORD smelled a sweet savour; and the LORD said in his heart . . .**

Notice the burnt offerings touched the heart of the holy God of Israel. And he says:

> **. . . I will not again curse the ground any more for man's sake; for the imagination of man's heart is evil from his youth; neither will I again smite any more every thing living, as I have done.**

So the burnt offering, the Bible tells us why God instituted burnt offerings. It is to touch His heart over man's sin nature. That's why they were instituted. There was no need for burnt offerings when God first created man. It was good, there was no sin. That's why, in fact, He said it was very good.

And now man sinned. And now God has provided a remedy. Because you notice, if you remember in Genesis 2:15, God told Adam and Eve, the day you sin you shall die thereof. There's a penalty for sin. And the burnt offerings are taking that penalty, temporarily atoning for the penalty, until it shall be taken away.

Again let me read Genesis 8:20–21:

And Noah builded an altar unto the LORD; and took of every clean beast, and of every clean fowl, and offered burnt offerings on the altar. And the LORD smelled a sweet savour; and the LORD said in his heart . . .

It touched the holy God of Israel.

. . . I will not again curse the ground any more for man's sake; for the imagination of man's heart is evil from his youth. . . .

So we see the foundation in the Torah for the reason, for the need of sacrifices. It's because of man's evil heart. It is because of man's evil nature.

And it affects God. God says, "I will stay judgment." That judgment should come, but because of the burnt offerings, it touches His heart and I will stay the judgments.

Now we come to Leviticus 16, the Day of Atonement. And when we come to the Day of Atonement it is even clearer what God is doing here, because we know that first on the Day of Atonement that the high priest had to offer a bullock for himself and his family for their sin. And he went in and sprinkled that on the Holy of Holies. And then he came back a second time, with actually the first part of a two phase sacrifice. He comes in with a goat whose blood is shed and he sprinkles that on the top of the altar—excuse me—on the top of the Ark of the Covenant, which is called in our terminology the Mercy Seat.

And look what happens when he does this In verse 21:

And Aaron shall lay both his hands upon the head of the live goat . . .

Excuse me, excuse me. Afterward, it is verse 16.

And he shall make an atonement for the holy place, because of the uncleanness of the children of Israel, and because of their transgressions in all their sins: and so shall he do for the tabernacle of the congregation, that remaineth among them in the midst of their uncleanness.
—Leviticus 16:16

So, the first goat is slain, the blood is brought into the Holy of Holies. And it is done because of the uncleanness that affects the temple. Then they go outside, Aaron, on the outside, So the children of Israel could see it:

And Aaron shall lay both his hands upon the head of the live goat, and confess over him all the iniquities of the children of Israel, and all their transgressions in all their sins, putting them upon the head of the goat, and shall send him away by the hand of a fit man into the wilderness: And the goat shall bear upon him all their iniquities unto a land not inhabited: and he shall let go the goat in the wilderness.
—Leviticus 16:21–22

Notice that the high priest confesses all the iniquities, transgressions, and sins. This is everything. This is willful sin. This is rebellious sin. This is unintentional sin. Iniquity, the Scriptures define iniquity; look how it is defined in Leviticus 18. This is iniquity:

> **Moreover thou shalt not lie carnally with thy neighbour's wife, to defile thyself with her. . . .**

Is adultery

> **And thou shalt not let any of thy seed pass through the fire to Molech . . .**

That's child sacrifice.

> **Thou shalt not lie with mankind, as with womankind . . .**

That's homosexuality

The next one is completely, totally vile. Verse 24:

> **Defile not ye yourselves in any of these things: for in all these the nations are defiled which I cast out before you: And the land is defiled: therefore I do visit the *iniquity* thereof upon it**
>
> —Leviticus 18:24–25

Iniquity. Do you remember on the Day of Atonement, the high priest laid his hands on the goat for iniquity. According to the Torah, iniquity is adultery, fornication, homosexuality, child killing, all sorts of iniquity. It is not just unintentional sin. The blood was needed for all sin on the Day of Atonement.

When we go back and we look at the end of the Day of Atonement, look what it says here in verse 30:

For on that day shall the priest make an atonement for you, to cleanse you, that ye may be clean from all your sins before the LORD.

Without that shed blood, without all the rituals on the Day of Atonement, God, the heart, the heart of the holy God of Israel can't be touched. The price for sin can't be paid.

And notice, that the children of Israel were clean after all the rituals on the Day of Atonement. And after that blood was sprinkled on the Holy of Holies. And the high priest laid his hands on that goat, and sent the goat off, the children of Israel were clean.

The blood was needed in Noah's day.

The blood was needed in Moses' day.

And the blood is needed today.

And if I get time to develop it, we'll see how Jesus of Nazareth shed His blood according to the Word of God, and paid that atonement so that we are now clean before the holy God of Israel.

Without the shed blood on the Day of Atonement we are unclean—both Jew and Gentile.

Praying is not. Aren't we to fast and try our soul on the Day of Atonement? Yes, that's part of it. But part of it is also that blood is to be shed, which the law requires before Moses.

In Noah's day, Noah was offering clean beasts unto the LORD because God initiated that when man fell.

And I think of Job, when Job's counselors—and we look at the end of Job 41—when his counselors gave him false counsel, what happened? It says, the LORD, the God of Israel told Job to offer bullocks for them, burnt offerings, because of their false counsel. God Himself, when we read in Job, told those false counselors to offer bullocks because of the sin that they had done.

We look at Abraham, when he went to offer Isaac in Genesis 22. He said to offer him as a burnt offering. They knew; Abraham knew what burnt offerings were. He knew the purpose of the burnt offerings.

Why? Because God had instituted it when man fell. And, and when God made the covenant with Abraham, Abraham got the bullock, sheep, goat, and other animals, and split them in half. And God, Abraham fell into a deep sleep and the God of Israel walked in the midst of them, because God initiates blood covenants with us.

The blood is very, very important.

Thank you

Rabbi Tovia Singer

The charge is that you can come to this synagogue. You can pray all you like. You can read from the holy Scriptures in the book of Psalms, but frankly, you don't have blood. And if you don't have the blood of Jesus you are lost. There is no hope for you.

You quoted Genesis 3 and then went to Genesis 8. I wanted to see if you went to Genesis 4 and you did not. In Genesis 4 we are told about the nature of man.

You say he is hopeless; Scriptures say otherwise. When God is addressing Cain in Genesis 4, He says that Satan, the evil inclination, is waiting for you. He's hiding behind the door. You are his desire, but you can master over him. In Christian theology this is impossible.

You went to Genesis 8, and began to talk about how Noah brought a sacrifice for sin in Genesis 8:20–21.

If you look at the Bible there is not a single word about sin in Genesis 8:20–21. In fact, animal sacrifices have nothing do about sin at all. In fact, if those sacrifices were for sin or uncleanliness, I'm surprised that sacrifice was not brought in Genesis 9, the next chapter when Noah becomes drunk, and [inaudible] his son, those who engage in sin. That would be the perfect time to bring sacrifices, if what Christianity demands of me is true.

Of course, nothing could be further from the truth. These sacrifices have nothing to do with sin.

Leviticus 16 we find these sacrifices, the blood that is sprinkled.

And then we find the fact that you have to, you have to, you have to pain your heart, in the sense of fasting and so on and repentance.

Interesting—in Leviticus 16 when it speaks about the sacrifice, it doesn't say it is forever. Only when it says you must oppress your soul, that is forever. Why is that?

The Bible tells us this, all we have to do is look at the delicious Scriptures; all you have to do is look. Look at what the prophet says.

King Solomon when he built the first temple, he addressed the issue. When King Solomon built the first temple, many—nearly three thousand—years ago, so King Solomon prophetically described what's going to happen when the Jews went into exile.

Listen carefully, remember he just built it. He's inaugurating the temple, 1 Kings 8:46–50. And he says these words, "One day you are going to be thrown out of the land of Israel. You're not going to have this temple. You're not going to be here in Jerusalem. You're going to be in the land of your enemy, be it far or be it near."

That's where we are right now. Whether we're in the United States, or the former Soviet Union, we are in exile.

And King Solomon is talking to you. And he says this, "When you are in exile, and you realize that you made a terrible mistake in your life, that you want to repent what should you do? You want those sins to go away."

Does it say there you should believe in Jesus, and know there is a cross and don't you know you need blood. Is the message of that Christian Bible articulated by King Solomon?

Oh no, listen to what [Rabbi uses Hebrews words] says. "When you are in the land of your enemies be it far of near, I want you to turn your face to this place." (That's why we as Jews we face Jerusalem when we pray, wherever we are.) "And you should confess your sin in heaven. God will hear your prayers. And will forgive you for all your transgressions."

Isn't it strange not a word about your sweet Jesus. Isn't it odd there's not a word about, you'll need blood—no, not a word at all. Why is this? Because in our exile there is no blood sacrifices at all.

In fact, you think about Job. In Christian theology what Job did when he was a righteous man and followed God in spite of the torment, He did not need any cross to save him. In fact, Job went through this great struggle and was able to conquer this inclination with all these tests on his own. In Christian theology, John, what Job did was impossible.

Let's think about King David. King David had made a devastating mistake in his life. And I use the word mistake lightly. King David, he calls it in Psalm 51, a blood transgression. Note the Talmud is not exactly as it appears in the *Tanakh*. But he did something terrible. And he is confronted by the prophet Nathan (2 Samuel 12).

And I know that some of us think in our lives, you know what, I did something terrible, I, I never even told my wife about what I've done. I never told my husband, my father, my best friend doesn't even know. And you wonder if God will ever look at you again.

Listen to what happened to [*Rabbi used Hebrew words*] . . .

(How much time do I have left—about four minutes? How much? A minute and half.)

He's confronted by the prophet Nathan over his sin. What does King David do? Does he say that I believe in Jesus? Does he run to an altar some place in Jerusalem? No. King David said these words— listen what came out of his, what he said: "I have sinned before the LORD." Nathan saw it was true repentance, and he said, "The LORD has already forgiven you."

No blood, no cross, no Calvary. No, no.

Now, you should know, and I'm going to do this in 60 seconds, that King David speaks about the fact, don't get obsessed with blood, don't get involved with, don't worry about sin sacrifices. In fact in Psalm 40:6–7, King David says, listen to this, "Sacrifice and offerings you did not desire, but my ears you have opened for me, because [*inaudible*] burnt offerings and sin offerings you didn't require."

Now do you think that the Church likes those words? Do you think that New Testament loves the word that God wants to know for us?

If you go to the book of Hebrews 10:5–6, Hebrews changes [*inaudible*] very nicely. But it says, "A body you have prepared for me."

How do you change my Bible? How does your Christian Bible change the Word of God? And if you are going to alter my Scriptures, you think I'm going to get baptized, destroy my relation with God and my people, over a Bible tampering.

Let's go back to the Scriptures.

Thank you

Part Two

Chaplain John McTernan

Okay, let's go back to the Scriptures. Let's see what David said. Let's go to Psalm 51 where David is addressing what the rabbi was saying (verse 17):

The sacrifices of God are a broken spirit: a broken and a contrite heart, O God, thou wilt not despise. Do good in thy good pleasure unto Zion: build thou the walls of Jerusalem.

Now look at how David answered:

Then shalt thou be pleased with the sacrifices of righteousness, with burnt offering and whole burnt offering: then shall they offer bullocks upon thine altar.

Of course David said you need blood sacrifices. The *Tanakh*, the Torah it is all through it, it's all through it. But the problem is, the rabbi doesn't have the sacrifices today.

And he is trying to dance around it. But, the Torah hasn't changed. He said that Leviticus—if I remember correctly rabbi—that Yom Kippur was not even an eternal statute. Leviticus 16:34:

And this shall be an everlasting statute unto you, to make an atonement for the children of Israel for all their sins once a year. And he did as the LORD commanded Moses.

The requirement for blood for sin on Yom Kippur was an everlasting statute. We looked at Genesis 8, and let me read this very carefully again because the rabbi didn't see sin in there.

And Noah builded an altar unto the LORD; and took of every clean beast, and of every clean fowl, and offered burnt offerings on the altar.

—Genesis 8:20

And look at the effect of the burnt offerings

And the LORD smelled a sweet savour; and the LORD said in his heart . . .

Remember the burnt offerings. This is the first time in the Bible, burnt offerings, sacrifices for sin or sacrifices are mentioned. And it says:

And the LORD smelled a sweet savour; and the LORD said in his heart, I will not again curse the ground any more for man's sake; for the imagination of man's heart is evil from his youth. . . .

—Genesis 8:21

There is sin, there is wickedness. Man's heart is wicked. And God saying that the burnt offerings are a sweet savor. And I will not again judge the earth, like He did for man's wickedness.

Genesis 4—lets go back to Genesis 4. And let's read Genesis 4:

And she again bare his brother Abel. And Abel was a keeper

> **of sheep, but Cain was a tiller of the ground. And in process of time it came to pass, that Cain brought of the fruit of the ground an offering unto the LORD. And Abel, he also brought of the firstlings of his flock and of the fat thereof. And the LORD had respect unto Abel and to his offering.**
>
> —Genesis 4:2–4

So Cain is bringing the sheep before the LORD. And the LORD honors Cain for what—excuse me—Abel for what Abel was doing.

> **But unto Cain and to his offering he had not respect. And Cain was very wroth, and his countenance fell.**
>
> —Genesis 4:5

Cain was upset because God would not accept the fruit. But God did accept the sheep that were brought to him.

> **And the LORD said unto Cain, Why art thou wroth? and why is thy countenance fallen? If thou doest well, shalt thou not be accepted?**
>
> —Genesis 4:6–7

Well, we know what well is. It is to bring the sheep like Cain did, like Abel did. That's what the "well" means, to follow what your brother did. And the proof of that is if you read on, it says that Cain became very angry with Abel because he didn't want to do what Abel did, to bring the sheep before the LORD. And we can see why, when we get to Genesis 8, we can see what happened with Noah.

And my time is up. Your turn.

Rabbi Tovia Singer

I, I, I only have. Shalom (moderator), how much time do I have in this segment? I have four minutes.

[Moderator]: Three

Even though I have three minutes, I am going to take a, I am going to take a little segment out of . . .

You need to understand his position. Very important you understand that he claims that Christianity—it's not John—it's Christianity claims that Judaism is defective.

The fact we don't have a blood sacrifice today means that obviously there's something wrong with your faith. There is blood, and that is the blood of Jesus. And you need that blood, and without that blood there is no atonement.

You have to go back to Scripture. What does the Bible say about this? In the book of Hosea 3:4–5, Hosea prophesied of our situation today.

He says the Jewish people, the children of Israel, will abide many day—no sacrifice, no king.

According to you we have a king—that's Jesus.

No sacrifice. According to you we have a sacrifice—that's Jesus.

No urim or thummim, no high priest—you say that's Jesus.

We will abide that way until the end of days, until the messianic age, until we return to David and God Himself in the messianic age.

Now listen to this, chapter 14: what do we do? What do we do through these years. We don't have a sacrificial system? Do we convert to Christianity and live a life without Sabbath, without God, without [inaudible] those precious commandments?

No, this is what Hosea says. Listen. These are the words of the prophet. What does the prophet say? He says these words, "Take with you words, words, not a cross, no. Take with you words. You say it every day, every day, and return to the LORD."

Listen to this, "and let us render for bulls, the offering of our lips."

[Rabbi speaks in Hebrew.]

"Let's us render for bulls the offering of your lips." That means instead of sacrifices, we are to pray. We follow precisely what the

Tanakh says. And that's why John I call upon you. I pray that one day too, you will repent of Christianity, and you are going to say you know what, I'm going to grab the shirt of a Jew, because we know that God is with you.

Part Three

Chaplain John McTernan

I would like to tie this all in, in three minutes, which is impossible. But I'd like to tie it in to show you Isaiah 53. I'm going keep this real brief.

It is not about Israel, but it is about the Messiah. Isaiah 53 is the bridge between the need of the blood, and what the Messiah is going to do.

Unfortunately I can't read these Scriptures. Perhaps on your own you can read them.

Rabbi Singer earlier mentioned Isaiah 11 was about the Messiah. At least parts of Isaiah 11. I totally agree with you. Then we get to Isaiah 42, and this is called Isaiah's Servant's Song. The First Servant Song, Isaiah 42:1–8 is about the Messiah. In fact when you look at verse 6:

I the LORD have called thee in righteousness, and will hold thine hand, and will keep thee, and give thee for a covenant of the people, for a light of the Gentiles.

You see the Messiah is not only meant for Israel. Of course, Israel is the vehicle Messiah is going to come through. But the Messiah is going to be for everybody in the world.

So we have the First Servant Song. It is about the Messiah. Then we go to Isaiah 49. And we will see that Isaiah 49 is not about Israel. Isaiah 49 is about the Messiah. And we get to verse 6:

And he said, It is a light thing that thou shouldest be my

servant to raise up the tribes of Jacob, and to restore the
preserved of Israel: I will also give thee for a light to the
Gentiles, that thou mayest be my salvation unto the end of
the earth.

Verse 8:

Thus saith the LORD, In an acceptable time have I heard
thee, and in a day of salvation have I helped thee: and I will
preserve thee, and give thee for a covenant of the people,
to establish the earth, to cause to inherit the desolate heri-
tages.

Isaiah 49 is a covenant, just like Isaiah 42 said, that the Messiah is
going to bring. It is not only for Israel, but it's for the Gentiles.

Then we get to Isaiah 50, which I do not have time to cover now.
But Isaiah 50, the Servant Song there is about the Messiah. So we have
three of the first four Servant Songs about the Messiah.

Then we come to Isaiah 52, starting at verse 13:

Behold, my servant shall deal prudently, he shall be exalted
and extolled, and be very high. As many were astonied at
thee; his visage was so marred more than any man, and his
form more than the sons of men.

Here is the connection with the two comings of the Messiah. He's going to be exalted, they are reversed though. He's going to be exalted,
but he's also going to be extremely marred. He's going to be more
than any man.

And when we read on in Isaiah 53, remember this is about the
LORD's Servant. The first three Servant Songs are about the Messiah.
The fourth Servant Song is about the Messiah. And we get here and it
tells you why the Messiah, what the covenant is.

> **He is despised and rejected of men; a man of sorrows, and acquainted with grief: and we hid as it were our faces from him; he was despised, and we esteemed him not. Surely he hath borne our griefs, and carried our sorrows: yet we did esteem him stricken, smitten of God, and afflicted.**
>
> —Isaiah 53:2–3

The Messiah was stricken, smitten and stricken of God, for our sins. He paid the price that was due for our sin.

> **But he was wounded for our transgressions, he was bruised for our iniquities: the chastisement of our peace was upon him; and with his stripes we are healed. All we like sheep have gone astray; we have turned every one to his own way; and the LORD hath laid on him the iniquity of us all.**

Remember what iniquity was? We talked about it earlier. "Of us all" There is a price to pay for sin.

And if Rabbi Singer does not want the price of the Messiah to pay for his sin then when he stands before the holy God of Israel, he's going to have to pay that price himself.

The Messiah has paid the price for sin. It is an awful price. Sin is terrible. He's the holy God of Israel. Who can stand in front of Him in their own righteousness, in their own holiness?

His holiness is beyond anything we can imagine. I could never, I could never stand in front of the holy God of Israel, never with the sin that I committed. But because what the Messiah did, because He was like a sheep led to the slaughter, He took the penalty for sin that I deserve.

I wish I could go on more, but rabbi it is up to you.

Rabbi Tovia Singer

Right, lets do this very quickly.

One might say, you know what, I can't speak for the LORD. I can't stand before Him. I'm a sinner. I'm lost. I am hopeless. And therefore I need some intercessor. I need some Jesus. I need Him to go. He has to die for me.

Is that what the Bible really says? Isaiah 55:6–7 speaks to you, John. "Seek the LORD when He is found, call on Him when He is near." And God says exactly this, if the wicked person turn away from his sinful thoughts, from his wicked deeds, God will forgive him.

You might say how can God forgive such a person? Listen to these words of the Almighty.

For my ways are higher than your ways, My thoughts are higher than your thoughts, as the heavens are higher than the earth, so to are my ways.

Don't try to figure God out. Don't say you can't forgive, we can't serve Him. I have the LORD of Lords, the hosts of hosts.

Because of you, John [*inaudible*], I can stand before the Almighty, and He will say He will forgive you, no blood, Jesus.

Let's talk about the servant. You say that this is all about the Messiah. Isn't that odd?

And you quote Isaiah 42 then go to 49. You should have—and I know this time won't permit—so I go through this real quick, and I hope you go through this on your own. Isaiah 41:8–9; 43:10–11; 44:4, 24; 45:20–21; 48:20; 49:3 all say explicitly that Israel is My servant. Not as you say the Messiah is God's Servant.

In fact the same Isaiah 42 you quote from, at the end of the chapter it says, "Who is blind but My servant."

Is your Messiah blind?

Now, I know how it goes that there is two different servants in Isaiah 42 and three servants here; this is not true.

You quoted from Isaiah 49. You said that Isaiah 49 is about the Messiah. John, your Christianity says that Isaiah 49 is about the Messiah.

I would just like to say what does Isaiah think? That's how I began this presentation. What's Isaiah's opinion? What does God say?

Hmm . . . open Isaiah 49, but don't start with verse 6, go to verse 3, what does it say? The prophet is standing and he is standing against your teachings. And he says, "but you Israel you are My servant."

I'll grant you this. If I have to choose between Isaiah and the cross, I have to choose between the Word of God and Jesus, I know who I'm going with. I'm going with the LORD of Lords, Host of hosts. And please God that we all should turn to *Hashem* in our lives, so it will bring about the true Messiah, come quickly in our time.

Thank you

Conclusion

Chaplain John McTernan

Let's go to the Scriptures. You can't, it's impossible to read the Scriptures without seeing the shed blood. You just can't gloss over it. You can look from Genesis which I showed you from the very beginning, and we can go all the ways through until the end, that there is a need for blood because it pays the price for sin.

Yes, we have to repent, but the rabbi, what he quoted in Isaiah 55—yes, that's true. But there is still a penalty to be paid.

It's like, what I hear is, all this which is true and we are going to forget what Moses said. We are going to forget about the temple. We are going to forget about the burnt offerings; we are going to forget about the peace offerings; we are going to forget about all that, because you don't have it. The rabbi doesn't have it. But it is needed.

I read to you Leviticus 16:34, where it is an everlasting statute, that you're clean before the holy God of Israel only when the blood has been shed. Of course there was more needed on the Day of Atonement. Of course there was repentance needed. Of course there was fasting needed. Of course there was afflicting the soul. That was all needed.

But the bottom line was the high priest had to go into to the Holy

Rabbi vs. Chaplain

of Holies with that shed blood for you to be clean before the holy God of Israel.

Continuing with Isaiah 53—I wish I could develop the four Servant Songs a little more—but let us look at Isaiah 53:

> **He was oppressed, and he was afflicted, yet he opened not his mouth: he is brought as a lamb to the slaughter, and as a sheep before her shearers is dumb, so he openeth not his mouth. He was taken from prison and from judgment: and who shall declare his generation? for he was cut off out of the land of the living: for the transgression of my people was he stricken.**
>
> —Isaiah 53:7–8

Jesus of Nazareth, the holy God of Israel, both man and God, was stricken for your sin so He could redeem you to Himself. The price for sin had to be paid. And if you pay it yourself, you've got to stand before the holy God of Israel on your own, in your own holiness and your own righteousness. And no one can do that.

Rabbi Tovia Singer

It is interesting throughout the Servant Songs the servant is identified numerous times. I know that most of you don't have Bibles here. I pray you'll look this up when you get home. And you'll turn to *Hashem* with all your heart.

When you understand Scripture, the servant is identified countless times throughout this text. Does anyone want to guess how many times the servant is called the Messiah throughout them? Zero, it doesn't exist. It only exists in the imagination of Christian leaders who wish to bring the Jewish people to Christianity.

As I mentioned earlier—and time doesn't allow to repeat myself— you go through the text of Isaiah 41 all the way through 49, every time the servant is Israel. In fact, Isaiah 52 and Isaiah 54 both are

55

speaking—and Christians agree with this—are speaking about Israel in the single.

Fifty-four is the famous [*Hebrew word*] read twice a year, where the servant is God's wife who is despised and rejected; the same thing we find in Isaiah 49. The promise of God is that God will never turn away from Israel, never turn away from the Jewish people. These are the very prophecies that make up the Jewish Scriptures.

And all you have to do is read it. I want to say this to you and, I probably have only about sixty seconds left. I am a *kohane*, I am a priest. I pray to God, that in time, in short time, that I could have the good fortune to bring sacrifices to the final temple. I hope that I will soon be in Jerusalem on the [*inaudible*] bringing sacrifices, because it is a beautiful thing. It's taking the mundane of the material and raising it up to God.

But the claim of the Church is, oh, no. Without sacrifices you're lost; without blood you have no hope here.

I ask you the question. Daniel who was a righteous, holy man with God called my friend. He didn't have any sacrifices. He lived during an exile, the Babylonian exile. How did he get to [*inaudible*] without the Yom Kippur sacrifices? How could he have been a prophet of God?

First you don't need it. Scripture tells us, clearly, that when you don't have the sacrifices you pray (Hosea 6:6; 14:3).

So all we do is this. We go to the Bible and we see what Scripture literally says. Then we say this, "Yeah, you know Christianity, very powerful religion, looks great." You know so many, but you know what, we have to choose God; you know what, regardless of how many friends I could have by being a Christian, I've got to choose my one true friend. That is the Almighty, blessed be His holy name. That's what the *Tanakh* is based on and that's what we are based on.

Thank you very much.

End of second debate

Chapter Three

Questions and Answers

Moderator

Thank you very much, wonderful audience. That concludes the second debate.

And we now open it up for the question and answer session. We invite questions from the audience. Please, when you ask your question, speak very loudly so I don't have to repeat the questions. And also if you kindly direct it to either of our two debaters or to both if you would like.

Question One

My question is basically, I didn't realize that in Christianity the core that they believe is that Messiah is the God of Israel which the gentlemen says. I'm not even going into the other question that they believe that Jesus Christ was Messiah.

My first question is, my basic disagreement is, how can something that I can't imagine be a God?

Chaplain John McTernan

Well, in responding to I guess it was a statement more than a question. Because you can't imagine it, does not mean God can't do it. It is the Word of God that is the final authority and not what you can imagine, and not what you can believe, right.

Well, let's look, let's go to Exodus 33. I'll read to you from the Scriptures here. And it says that Moses wanted to see the glory of the

God of Israel. I believe in Exodus when I read it, that this is literal. I don't take this figurative. I think Exodus is a historical event, that it happened. The God of Israel literally gave, Moses heard the God of Israel with his ears.

Okay, I believe that.

So with that, let's take a look at what the Scriptures says in Exodus 33. We will start at verse 20:

> **And he said, Thou canst not see my face: for there shall no man see me, and live.**

God says seeing Him means to look into His face.

> **And the LORD said, Behold, there is a place by me, and thou shalt stand upon a rock: And it shall come to pass, while my glory passeth by, that I will put thee in a clift of the rock, and will cover thee with my hand while I pass by: And I will take away mine hand, and thou shalt see my back parts: but my face shall not be seen.**
>
> —Exodus 33:21–23

Now I take that literal. I see no reason why not to take that literal. And the holy God of Israel stood before Moses, or Moses stood before the holy God of Israel, and He wanted to look into God's face. God said, You can't look into my face with the glory and live, so I'm going to hide you. But you can see My form as I pass by.

So I believe that as God revealed Himself to Moses, that the holy God of Israel has a form that we can recognize. I don't know if that directly answers your question, but I think it kind of gets close to what you were, what you were saying.

Rabbi Tovia Singer

You know, the Bible says that God will not forsake the Jewish people, on the wings of eagles. Does that mean that God is a chicken? (Are these jokes too complicated for this section over here?)

This is called anthropomorphism. That God uses the language that we, man, understands in order to communicate with us.

Let's talk about, "Hear oh Israel, the LORD is our God, the LORD is one."

These are the first words that a Jewish child learns as a babe. When a Jew is 120 and it is time, to stand before the LORD of lords and the Host of hosts, the last words on the lips of a Jew. You say we can't imagine, but God says in Numbers 23:19 that God is not a man that He should lie. He is not mortal that He should repent. The exact same message is repeated in 2 Samuel 15:29.

I'm keeping these answers compact for you. The Bible tells us how to worship God. There is not a single scripture anywhere in *Tanakh* that says there is one God but three, three in one. It doesn't exist.

If you want to find that, you'll find it in the Council of Nicea, the Council of Constantinople. It's not of God; it's idolatry. And therefore a Jew has to be prepared to give his life, rather than believe these idolatrous words.

I'll stop there.

Moderator

The words of another wonderful speaker Dennis Preager. He always asks for questions and alternative speeches. Let's see if we can keep these as concise questions so we can get as many people asking as possible.

Question Two

Is it possible [*inaudible*] that the writers of the New Testament, they knew the Old Testament, right, the Jewish Bible. They read the Jewish Bible and say okay, there is a prophecy here so write it and make it sound like Jesus is this guy here. Because you're writing after the fact. There is a reading Jewish Bible. You read a prophecy, right, and they write it so it sounds like they are linked.

Rabbi Tovia Singer
Since you went first, I'll just make this brief comment on that.

I don't know, I only deal with and I make claims and make statements upon what is black and white and absolutely certain. So much is at stake. I generally never. I never, I always stay away from speculation.

It appears to me however, that Matthew, the author of the first Gospel, sort to do that . . . sort to look at the Jewish Scriptures, and look at Jesus and mold Him as much as he possibly could in these texts. Of course Matthew will therefore be the greatest failure of the New Testament, because he will alter our text, change our Scriptures, in order to make it look Christological.

In fact, I believe this, and I'll end with this, that if Matthew and we don't know who wrote Matthew, but whoever wrote it, if that book had never existed, many more Jews would have been lost to Christianity, because he made the effort to manipulate our text and shape the life of Jesus in a way that would be appreciative to Jews. The Jewish people gave their lives, rather than convert to Christianity, because he made it implausible. Okay.

Chaplain John McTernan
The only thing that I can say, is that I believe the New Testament. Gospel writers were eyewitnesses. They were eyewitness accounts. They were not forcing anything. They were writing things as they saw them. So I don't know if that answers your question.

Question Three
Now, my question is to you is that [*the rest of the question is inaudible*].

Chaplain John McTernan
You mentioned the Talmud and I know nothing about the Talmud. [*Inaudible*].

Rabbi Tovia Singer

Let me, let me, I think what he is asking John and you correct me if I'm wrong and summarize it, what this gentlemen is saying, for a very long time the Church has not permitted the laity, the people, to study the Bible on their own.

And his question is essentially, what were they hiding? Why didn't they allow a lay person to have access to Scripture, to have access to the original, in a proper English translation?

I know this sounds strange, but I want to say this if I may, John . . .

Chaplain McTernan

Is that your question?

Rabbi Singer

Yeah. Just so you understand that John is part of a Christian, a path that really disagrees with this completely. I say this in defense of him. In fact John would definitely oppose this.

That is the Roman Catholic Church who has for more than a thousand years, people couldn't even own a Bible, and the first translators of the Bible, William Tyndale, John Rogers, and others, were executed and burned at the stake for committing this.

But John, because it is very important, for I don't speak for him, but I just did and it is so important, that he is an evangelical Christian Protestant who completely rejects this and opposes this. And the Protestants want the laity to read the Bible and study the Scripture.

It is the Catholic Church that said we are going to keep it in Latin. No one can understand except the priests. And, John, I'm sorry, I didn't mean to [*inaudible*]. Sometimes as Jews we don't understand all the nuances. How did I do?

Chaplain McTernan

I would like to add just a little bit to this.

I can understand that Christianity may appear to be very confusing to you. And rabbi tried to show, he is very astute on the different nuances, but as many, I can't compare the numbers, but huge numbers of people like me perished to get this Bible in our language—huge numbers—burnt at the stake, killed, drowned, impaled. You name it, it happened to us, like your people suffered. So, we could get this Bible in our language to study.

And one other thing, what we call the Old Testament, the *Tanakh*, comes directly from the Masoretic Text, the Ben Hayyim text.

When we went to translate this into English, we went to the Hebrews, the rabbis, back in the 1500s and we got their Masoretic Text. And this King James text comes directly from the rabbis in the 1500s. It is called the Ben Hayyim manuscript. Did I pronounce that right?

Rabbi Singer
Yeah, I just would say this. The rabbis are here to tell you that it is not the correct manuscript today. That, in fact the critical text, in the King James Version

Chaplain McTernan
Maybe the rabbis are wrong, maybe the rabbis are wrong, and the ancient rabbis are right.

Rabbi Singer
If we were wrong now, we are wrong then. I would say this to you, the Church unfortunately has changed the text of the Masoretic text, but I don't want to get into in this.

Go ahead. Shalom.

Chaplain McTernan
I don't want to get into it either.

Question Four
My question is to the Christian.

Do you believe that the five books of Moses is the Word of God?

And if you do, it says numerous places that these laws are for ever and ever for all generations, and many place and many laws.

What is your response to that?

Chaplain John McTernan

Yes, I believe the Torah. I think I mentioned it earlier that the Torah was directly given to Moses. He heard the word of the LORD and wrote it down.

Now your question about the Torah being eternal. It's eternal, but also when we look at the prophets, there is a New Covenant.

And I challenge you to look at Ezekiel, and especially the law of the temple, which I would have loved to get into, but I didn't. And I'll give you one example when you look at the law of the temple. There's steps on the altar. When you look in Exodus, when the altar under the law of Moses steps are forbidden. There is a contradiction there, and I believe that contradiction is explained by the New Covenant, which I don't have time to go into.

Yes, I believe the law of Moses is eternal. It was given literally by the holy God of Israel to Moses. And, I believe there is a New Covenant, coming after the covenant with Moses, which we can see the New Covenant in the law of the temple.

Rabbi Tovia Singer

I have to comment because I think the question is really excellent.

These are the words, I'd like to quote. Deuteronomy 29:30 says this:

The secret things belong to the LORD, but that which has been revealed belongs to us, and our children forever that we may keep all the words of this Torah.

So when he asks the question, obviously you believe in the five books of Moses as the Word of God. Do you follow it? Scripture says that the Torah is forever. That means every commandment is forever, yet it must be made clear, your religion says that every person in this room, you don't have to keep Sabbath, you don't eat kosher, you don't have to keep the law of Moses.

So again we have this staggering interesting confrontation. We have God on one side that says the commandments are forever. We have Ezekiel's prophecy, Ezekiel 36, 44 throughout 37, that the Jews are going to keep the [*Hebrew word*] during the messianic age.

And yet we have Christianity on the other hand that opposes the will of God, and frankly, if I have to choose between God and the Church, I choose the Almighty.

Question Five

You mentioned Isaiah and how it quotes My servant. You said it was messianic verse. Now you, yourself, said that Jesus is God and God is Jesus. Now which is the Servant here?

Chaplain McTernan

Yes, what happens, He's referred to as the suffering Servant. He was . . .

Questioner

God Himself took upon Himself the suffering Servant?

Chaplain McTernan

He had to be a man. He had to take on the seed of Abraham to redeem us. Otherwise we have to stand on our own before Him in judgment. So, that is the whole essence.

Yes, He's the Servant. He is God's Servant also.

Questioner

He is God and the Servant, too?

Rabbi Tovia Singer

You're asking a very, very good question. I'm not going to interrupt. I'm just going to say, your question is breathtaking. They, you have to go through a theological somersault in order to believe the Messiah is God and believe that Isaiah 53 is speaking of Messiah, because in Isaiah 53, God speaks about giving the Servant things, a promise of long life and a seed. How could God promise long life to God?

God is eternal He has no beginning and no end. How could God be subordinate to Himself? And I say this, that Christians are in . . . I don't know how you deal with this, because it requires this kind of circus act. That God, but He is also His Servant. And, God is. God is God of the universe. He serves no one. The world serves Him alone.

That was a great question.

Chaplain McTernan
Rabbi, I didn't finish, rabbi. I'll answer that to you from Psalm 110. Psalm 110, starting at verse one:

> **The LORD said unto my Lord, Sit thou at my right hand, until I make thine enemies thy footstool.**

So the LORD—in English we would say Jehovah—but Yahweh, said to my Lord—that's David's Lord—excuse me with the Hebrew *Adon*, which means servant. And he goes to say:

> **The LORD shall send the rod of thy strength out of Zion: rule thou in the midst of thine enemies. Thy people shall be willing in the day of thy power . . .**

This is all speaking about God's *Adon*. We get to verse 5:

> **The Lord at thy right hand shall strike through kings in the day of his wrath.**

Here we have a reverse. Here we have *Adonai* at the hand of Yahweh,

Jehovah. When you read Psalm 110, it's a perfect explanation that the Messiah, who is David's Lord, David has no Lord other than the God of Israel. David is the king of Israel. He has no other Lord than the God of Israel. But He is referring . . . David is referring to "my Lord." And, it says here shall sit at my right hand until thy enemies, until thine enemies, excuse me:

> **The LORD said unto my Lord, Sit thou at my right hand, until I make thine enemies thy footstool.**

And verse 5 says:

> **The Lord at thy right hand shall strike through kings in the day of his wrath.**

So what you have when you read Psalm 110, you have God sitting at the right hand of God. And that's exactly what Christians believe.

I hope that answered your question.

Rabbi Singer
I just have one point here. You know if you read the King James Version, that's what you come up with. "The LORD said to my Lord." Look in your King James. Except for the fact one is completely upper case and the other isn't. The same exact word. You know, but in the original Hebrew it's two entirely different words.

Chaplain McTernan
I said that, rabbi.

Rabbi Singer
Actually, you didn't. You said it to some point. You didn't say the whole thing, and this is important.
Chaplain McTernan

Adon. I used the word *Adon*.

Rabbi Singer

But, that's not what it says.

The word there is *la adonee*. And *la adonee* in the Bible is never about God. In fact, you take out a computer concordance. I think there was one here. And you look up word *adonee*, and in each and every case it appears with one exception, it refers to a human being like to Asap and others.

Now why does your Bible hide the fact that the word *adonee* is being used, meaning my servant lower case lower case "L." This Bible and all the other Christian Bibles that claim they consulted with rabbis before they translated. Why did they alter the word of God?

One other point about how this is taken. Psalm 110 was written by David not for himself to read. Read it. It was written as a psalm, meaning a song to be read in the temple, by the [*Hebrew word*] by those who would serve there. And the [*Hebrew word*] would say that the LORD (that means God) spoke to my lord, that means lower case "L" meaning King David.

But why does your Bible say, LORD, Lord?

Someone reading that would think it must mean that same word. I'm going to worship Jesus. There is nothing that could be further from the truth.

Chaplain McTernan

Can I respond to that, because he asked me a question?

Rabbi, I tried to find the scriptures and I can't, but that word that you mentioned is also found in Leviticus and Malachi. I believe Leviticus, Zechariah 3, refers to the God of Israel.

Rabbi Singer

No, never.

Chaplain McTernan

Okay, I'm not going to argue with you. We are going to Psalm 110:

The LORD said unto my Lord . . .

You are absolutely right, I agree with you that the second Lord is a man there. And the reason it is capitalized in the King James because when you go to verse 5, it says:

The Lord at thy right hand shall strike through kings in the day of his wrath.

Adonai at Your right hand. *Adonai* at Jehovah's right hand, shall strike through King's in the day of His wrath.

I asked you to read it in context. I asked you to look at the Scriptures, and you'll see exactly what I'm saying. In the first verse the word Lord there is a man. In the second, verse 5, when you read it, He's *Adonai,* at the right hand of Jehovah.

And that answers your question, where the Messiah is both God and man.

Read Psalm 110:1–5, and you'll see that the Messiah is at the right hand of Jehovah. And then in verse 5 you'll see that *Adonai* is at the right hand of Jehovah. I hope that answers your question.

Rabbi Singer

It is not that word *Adonai.* Again, it is not that word *Adonai*; it's the word *adonee.* It must be in all cases of not, of not sacred, but rather profane. Just do a search on it. I'll plug it. I cover this in my book. It, it every single text where that word appears it's always for a fact.

It breaks my heart. It's like a knife in my heart, watch your King James put a capital letter "L" where there is no such thing even as a capital letter in the Hebrew Bible.

How do they dare play with my Bible, alter it to make it look like it is speaking about Jesus. It blows my mind away.

Chaplain McTernan

I just explained it rabbi. If you read verse 5, you will see. Do you have your Bible there?

Rabbi Singer
Yeah, but I don't . . .

Chaplain McTernan
Okay, read verse 5 in the Hebrew. It shall say, "*Adonai* at thy right hand shall strike through kings in the day of His wrath." *Adonai* is at the right hand of Yahweh. That's why they capitalized it.

Rabbi Singer
It actually does not say those words. It doesn't say that God is at the right hand of God. It doesn't say thou shall strike down the enemies. What happens, these are interpolations, inserted words that simply don't exist.

I would just say, look at Scripture and one other point. Frankly, if these texts somehow are about Jesus, whose enemies of Israel should be struck down, how could Jesus be the Messiah?

Rome struck down the Jewish people. The Jews were in exile for two thousand years. This is a testimony that Jesus can't be the Messiah, because theoretically if this is talking about the Messiah, He has failed at the most basic task of destroying the enemies of Israel.

I say this unto you, the Messiah is not yet here. He will be here soon and He and He will destroy Hamas. And He will destroy the PLO. And He will destroy the United Nations. And He will destroy the European Union [*inaudible*] that has not come yet.

Note: Chaplain McTernan's response was eliminated from this section of the DVD. This DVD was produced by Rabbi Singer and he could offer no explanation of why this section of the debate was missing.
Question Six

Note: The first part of this question is missing from this DVD. The question was originally directed to Rabbi Singer, who deferred to Chaplain McTernan. The question was to explain the Branch of David.

Questioner
If you just mention it again. He wants to hear your response to it.

Chaplain McTernan
Sure, when we go, look at Jeremiah 23. Let's read Jeremiah 23. Now the Branch is mentioned about six times in the *Tanakh*. But, to save time, I will just go with this verse, Jeremiah 23, starting with verse 5:

> **Behold, the days come, saith the LORD, that I will raise unto David a righteous Branch, and a King shall reign and prosper, and shall execute judgment and justice in the earth. In his days Judah shall be saved, and Israel shall dwell safely: and this is his name whereby he shall be called, THE LORD OUR RIGHTEOUSNESS.**

So here is a title or reference to King Messiah. He is called the Branch. A righteous Branch shall be raised up unto David, who I believe this is a reference to the Messiah.

Now when we go to Zechariah 6, and we are talking the high priest is being referred to now. The prophet Zechariah is talking only to the high priest of Israel, and he's making a reference to him and he says:

> **Then take silver and gold, and make crowns, and set them upon the head of Joshua the son of Josedech, the high priest; And speak unto him, saying, Thus speaketh the LORD of hosts, saying, Behold the man whose name is The BRANCH. . . .**

So now the Messiah, as, high priest of Israel is standing in front of the prophet, and the prophet Zechariah is referring to him as the Branch, and he gives these messianic scriptures.

So what you have here is a blending of the Branch being from David, and now the high priest of Israel is being referred to as the Branch. And that's why I said the Messiah it merges. Both the high priest and the king of Israel merge together in the Messiah.

So does that answer?

Questioner
[*Inaudible*]

Rabbi Singer
This is something that I've gone through. If you study the Scriptures, those who represent the will of God are called god in the Bible. A person who doesn't have that understanding, that doesn't have that knowledge, it becomes a very complicated issue. It is interesting that even in the Christian Bible this is well understood.

In John 10:30–31 there's an interesting conversation between Jesus and people who were there. And He said, doesn't it say, in verse 31 I believe, doesn't say in your law that you are gods. That's Jesus talking.

In response to a confrontation that maybe Jesus claimed that He was God, and being stoned for this act. But if you look at this response as John plays in out, it is so obvious that John didn't dream for a moment that Jesus was God.

The way the story that is portrayed is that Jesus quoting from the book of Psalms where it refers to judges. Now the reason why this is important is that judges, are those who teach the will of God, and therefore they are called god. And as a result of that it is so clear, even as I mentioned earlier the New Testament never claims that Jesus is God.

Now of course you can look at John 1, and other texts that are ambiguous, and Christians seek to interpret it that way. But the clear text of the Bible is that the world will be changed, as a result of the coming of the Messiah.

You quoted Jeremiah which talks about how Judah will remain safe. Let's talk about Judah for a moment. Cause Judah, we'll talk about the Gaza strip, Gush Katiff, Gush Katiff doesn't look very safe to me right now, does it to you? It was destroyed, it was wiped out, as prophesied in Zephaniah 2. And Askolom the Bible would be next, and now it is under the threat of missile attacks. Judah is not dwelling safely. It's loaded with rockets and missiles ready to destroy Israel. Amona was just wiped out.

Are we living safely? Is this world are we living in a messianic age? Hardly.

Question Seven

Mr. McTernan, First of all question number one. How is it possible—I don't want to get too in depth obviously because of time pressing—but how could one consider believing and living a life of trust in this human being that the Christian religion doesn't even admit to the fact there was a time of conception. There is no Father in the picture. That's one.

Question number two is, if believing in God is a very lofty spiritual experience, how could that experience be attributed to a human being with flesh and blood?

Question number three is, if this is the world where people of the Christian faith believe He is the Messiah and this is the era of Messiah, how is it possible that with all that we see, if corruption, and unfaithfulness, stealing that is going around, dishonesty and all the more so of other things taken place, how can you claim that this is the era of Messiah you are living in?

Chaplain McTernan

Okay, I'm going to answer the third question and maybe I'll remember the first two.

It might be a matter of definition, but I won't call this the Messiah's era. When I look at Scriptures, I would call this the Church age. It is the period of time between the first coming of the Messiah and the second coming of the Messiah. We look at scriptures where it says that is God is working to make the Jews and Gentiles one in the Messiah.

There is a certain time period. This is limited to a certain time period. In fact the scriptures clearly limit it regarding Jerusalem, regarding Israel. The restoration of Israel shows according to the Bible that the Church age is coming to an end.

The period you're talking about is when the Messiah returns. I believe it is the second coming of the Lord Jesus. When He returns He's setting up a kingdom on earth here in Jerusalem.

And when you look at scriptures—look at Daniel 7—and you'll see the Messiah is returning with the clouds of Heaven.

Just look a couple of Scriptures up before that and you'll see that before the holy God of Israel, there is an innumerable host of people. It says thousands times thousands and ten thousands times ten thousands. I believe those are the redeemed in the Messiah that are returning with Him to establish His kingdom on earth.

I hope that answers your question. It might be a matter of terminology, but I don't view this as the messianic era. I view this as the Church era. The messianic era is yet to come.

Now there were two other questions.

Moderator
We will go over one of them. Because one of them I think you answered before and that is genealogy. Jesus has no father and [*inaudible*] genealogical line.

Chaplain McTernan
Oh, that was the question.

He has a Father. The only God of Israel is His Father. When you look at scriptures, the Messiah's Father is the holy God of Israel. That's who His Father is.
Rabbi Singer

I just, this is an important question I think because it says in the book of Numbers that the way you determine someone's tribal identification is [*Hebrew words*] according to the family, their father's house.

So when Christianity will claim that Jesus was born of a virgin, was conceived from a virgin, meaning that she lacked a human Jewish father from the house of David, there's no human father there, then Jesus is automatically disqualified from being the Messiah, because it is the father alone that transmits the genealogy.

And this was not an issue lost on the writers of the Christian Bible. The very first verse of the entire New Testament tries to address this. "This is the genealogy of Jesus Christ, David's son, no, son of Judah, son of David." Well, Abraham and David. And then what happens is, it traces that genealogy to Joseph. Well, Joseph, according to Matthew 1:23, is irrelevant, because Joseph wasn't Jesus' father, and therefore, Jesus can't possibly be the Messiah, and what you're worshipping is an error.

Chaplain McTernan

This is a whole debate topic in itself. Maybe I'll challenge Rabbi Singer on this. I challenge you to look at the genealogy of Israel's Messiah.

[*Break in the recording which eliminated part of Chaplain McTernan's remarks. I had made a statement that if Jesus of Nazareth was not Israel's King Messiah then Israel could not have one. I went then to explain why. The recording picks up with me explaining why Israel can't have a Messiah without the virgin birth.*]

Jeremiah 22, you'll see there's a curse put on his line, that no one from his seed is ever going to be the King of Israel. When you go into Isaiah 39, you will see that all the sons of Hezekiah were going to be made eunuchs in Babylon, because of what Hezekiah did, bringing the Babylonian emissaries into the treasury.

When you look at Jeremiah 52, you will see that King Zedekiah, all his sons were killed at Riblah. So the messianic line which is found in 1 Chronicles 3 either had a curse on it, it ended through all the king's son's being killed, or they were made eunuchs in Babylon.

And I believe that's why God set that up that the messianic line ended, and that only through the virgin birth of Jesus of Nazareth, can the Messiah come forth.

And that would be an excellent topic Rabbi Singer, we could go into.

Rabbi Singer
It would be. Just a little point here. If, in fact, Jeconiah's cursed, and there is no ability for there to be another king, how was there another king? You had [*Hebrew word*] where did he come from?

Chaplain McTernan
Who?

Rabbi Singer
Zedekiah.

Chaplain McTernan
Zedekiah, all his sons were killed at Riblah.

Rabbi Singer
I know, but just as an example Zedekiah was his uncle.

Chaplain McTernan
Yes.

Rabbi Singer
So that means that you have this huge line of folks who are coming straight down.

All you have to be eligible to be the Messiah, and there are people in this room right now who are eligible to be the Messiah, based on your genealogy is you have to be a descendent of King Solomon.

You are looking at a certain family tree here and tree here, saying these trees don't work. Isn't it odd as you look at the book of Matthew, it traces Jesus' genealogy through Jeconiah; Luke tries to hide it and it doesn't work in chapter 3. The truth is that the genealogy requires a theological somersault, a circus act in order to say that Jesus is the Messiah, It just doesn't work.

Chaplain McTernan

I addressed that the only genealogy for the Messiah, you can say there are millions, but it is limited to 1 Chronicles 3. That's the messianic line coming from David. And there is a curse on that line. It ended with the Babylonian captivity with Zedekiah, and all Hezekiah's descendents were made eunuchs. So that ended the line.

Rabbi Singer

So why give the genealogy altogether? See, if you're saying that the genealogy, that there is no human genealogy possible for the Messiah. It had to come from a virgin, why give us the genealogy, a cursed genealogy, which if you are from that genealogy as you say, you can't even be the Messiah. Why does Matthew even offer that's absolutely meaningless?

Chaplain McTernan

I don't know. Well, I don't know. I'll have to think about that.

End of the debate

Chapter Four

Postscript

During the debate, time is limited in responding to your opponents statements. There were seven statements of Rabbi Singer which need to be addressed. The following are responses that could not be made during the debate.

Rabbi Singer and Job's suffering

During the second debate in part one, Rabbi Singer said the following:

> In fact, you think about Job. In Christian theology what Job did, when he was a righteous man, and followed God in spite of the torment, He did not need any cross to save him. In fact, went through this great struggle, and was able to conquer this inclination, with all these tests on his own. In Christian theology, John, what Job did was impossible.

Chaplain McTernan's post–debate response

The Scriptures reveal, during Job's great suffering, what was the great inner strength that sustained him during the ordeal. It was the belief that His redeemer was coming, and that he would be resurrected from the dead. Job endured his suffering as he was looking for the coming of the Lord Jesus and the resurrection.

For I know that my redeemer liveth, and that he shall stand

at the latter day upon the earth: And though after my skin worms destroy this body, yet in my flesh shall I see God: Whom I shall see for myself, and mine eyes shall behold, and not another; though my reins be consumed within.
—Job 19:25–27

Job wanted his friends and everyone to know what was his strength to endure the suffering.

Oh that my words were now written! oh that they were printed in a book! That they were graven with an iron pen and lead in the rock for ever!
—Job 19:23–24

Rabbi Singer on the exiled Jews on what to do without the temple
He used 1 Kings 8:46–50 to show there was no need for sacrifices and blood atonement today. The rabbi said the following during the second debate, part one:

King Solomon when he built the first temple, he addressed the issue, what. When King Solomon built the first temple many— nearly three thousand—years ago, so King Solomon prophetically described what's going to happen when the Jews went into exile. Listen carefully, remember he just built it. He's inaugurating the temple, 1 Kings 8:46–50. And he says these words, one day you are going to be thrown out of the land of Israel. You're not going to have this temple. You're not going to be here in Jerusalem. You're going to be in the land of your enemy, be it far or be it near.

Chaplain McTernan's post debate response
The context of this section of Scripture is when Solomon dedicated the temple to the LORD. He is directing these verses to soldiers going

into battle. It has nothing to do with the temple and priesthood being destroyed and the entire nation being lead into captivity. It has to do with assuring captured soldiers, that God will not forsake them.

There is no indication from these verses that it is prophetic about Jerusalem and the temple being destroyed. All indications are that the temple is still functioning, and these verses are just for soldiers taken captive. The rabbi took these verses out of context to try and fit them into the present situation of the Jews.

If thy people go out to battle against their enemy, whither-soever thou shalt send them, and shall pray unto the LORD toward the city which thou hast chosen, and toward the house that I have built for thy name . . . If they sin against thee, (for there is no man that sinneth not,) and thou be angry with them, and deliver them to the enemy, so that they carry them away captives unto the land of the enemy, far or near; Yet if they shall bethink themselves in the land whither they were carried captives, and repent, and make supplication unto thee in the land of them that carried them captives, saying, We have sinned, and have done perversely, we have committed wickedness; And so return unto thee with all their heart, and with all their soul, in the land of their enemies, which led them away captive, and pray unto thee toward their land, which thou gavest unto their fathers, the city which thou hast chosen, and the house which I have built for thy name: Then hear thou their prayer and their supplication in heaven thy dwelling place, and maintain their cause, And forgive thy people that have sinned against thee, and all their transgressions wherein they have transgressed against thee, and give them compassion before them who carried them captive, that they may have compassion on them.

—1 Kings 8:44–50

Rabbi Singer and Hosea 14:1–2

The rabbi used these verses to show that there is no need for sacrifices today. He made this statement in debate two, part two:

> Now listen to this, chapter 14, what do we do? What do we do through these years, we don't have a sacrificial system? Do we convert to Christianity and live a life without Sabbath, without God, without [*inaudible*], those precious commandments? No this is what Hosea says, listen, These are the words of the prophet. What does the prophet say? He says these words, Take with you words, words, not a cross, no. Take with you words. You say it every day, every day, and return to the LORD. Listen to this, and let us render for bulls, the offering of our lips. [*Rabbi speaks in Hebrew*] Let's us render for bulls the offering of your lips. That means instead of sacrifices, we are to pray.

Chaplain McTernan's post debate response

The rabbi used Hosea 14:1–2 as the verses for the Jews to follow today without the temple. These verses follow:

> **O Israel, return unto the LORD thy God; for thou hast fallen by thine iniquity. Take with you words, and turn to the LORD: say unto him, Take away all iniquity, and receive us graciously: so will we render the calves of our lips.**
>
> —Hosea 14:1–2

Hosea lived around 700 B.C. and was a contemporary of Isaiah. At the time of Hosea the temple was still standing and was not to be destroyed until 586 B.C. The prophet does not supersede the law of Moses. The law of Moses was very clear that the sacrifices and sprinkled blood during Yom Kippur was the way all iniquity was taken away. The temple was standing in Hosea's day and this verse has nothing to do with eliminating animal sacrifices for sin. There is no prophetic aspect of this verse that can be applied to today. The rabbi's use of Hosea 14:1–2 was completely out of context and unsustainable.

Rabbi Singer and Isaiah 49:3 is about Israel

During the second debate in part three, the rabbi states that the servant of Isaiah 49:3 is Israel and not the Messiah:

> You quoted from Isaiah 49. You said that Isaiah 49 is about the Messiah. John, your Christianity says that Isaiah 49 is about the Messiah. I would just like to say what does Isaiah think? That's how I began this presentation. What's Isaiah opinion, what does God say? Hum, open Isaiah 49, But don't start with verse 6, go to verse 3, what does it say? The prophet is standing and he is standing against your teachings. And he says, but you Israel you are My servant.

Chaplain McTernan's post debate response

Isaiah 49:3 is an interesting verse as God identifies King Messiah as Israel My Servant. God is speaking to the Branch of David in the name of Israel, indicating through King Messiah, that God will be glorified:

> **And said unto me, Thou art my servant, O Israel, in whom I will be glorified.**
>
> —Isaiah 49:3.

The context of this song shows the nation of Israel cannot be the subject. King Messiah is the subject. Just a few verses later, the Servant of verse three is the one who restores Jacob to the LORD. The one who God formed in the womb to be His Servant is the one who redeems Jacob. The Servant of verse 3 has to be a person; otherwise, Israel brings Israel back to God.

This concept carries into verse 6. The Servant of verse 3 is again referred to as God's Servant. The ministry of this Servant is to raise up the tribes of Jacob and restore the people of Israel. Once again, the Servant of verse 3 has to be a person or the tribes of Jacob are raising up the tribes of Jacob. The context of the Second Servant Song demands that God's Servant found in verse 3 is a person and not the nation of Israel. The verses to show this follow:

> **And now, saith the LORD that formed me from the womb to be his servant, to bring Jacob again to him, Though Israel be not gathered, yet shall I be glorious in the eyes of the LORD, and my God shall be my strength. And he said, It is a light thing that thou shouldest be my servant to raise up the tribes of Jacob, and to restore the preserved of Israel.**
> —Isaiah 49:5–6

Rabbi Singer on Isaiah 55:5–8

The rabbi used these verses in an attempt to prove there was no need for an intercessor between man and the holy God of Israel. A sinner just turns away from sin and God then forgives the sin. During the second debate in part three, Rabbi Singer said the following:

> I can't speak for the LORD. I can't stand before Him. I'm a sinner. I'm lost. I am hopeless. And therefore I need some intercessor. I need some Jesus. I need Him to go. He has to die for me. Is that what the Bible really says? Isaiah 55:6–7 speaks to you John. Seek the LORD when He is found, call on Him when He is near. And God says exactly this, if the wicked person turn away from his sinful thoughts, from his wicked deeds, God will forgive him. You might say how can God forgive such a person? Listen to these words of the Almighty. For my ways are higher than your ways, My thoughts are higher than your thoughts, as the heavens are higher than the earth, so to are my ways.

Chaplain McTernan's post debate response

Isaiah 55:6-8 follows:

> **Seek ye the LORD while he may be found, call ye upon him while he is near: Let the wicked forsake his way, and the unrighteous man his thoughts: and let him return unto the LORD, and he will have mercy upon him; and to our God, for he will abundantly pardon. For my thoughts are not your thoughts, neither are your ways my ways, saith the LORD.**
>
> —Isaiah 55:6–8

When Isaiah wrote these words the temple was still standing. These verses say nothing about a time in the future when the priesthood and temple were destroyed all a person has to do is forsake sin and God will abundantly pardon.

Isaiah states, "and let him return unto the LORD." For a person to return to God, he would have to follow Yom Kippur. This person needs to afflict his soul for the sin on this day and then realize the animals died and paid the penalty for his sin: then this person becomes clean before the holy God of Israel. This is the requirements of the law of Moses needed to "return unto the LORD" and have God abundantly pardon sin.

> **And this shall be a statute for ever unto you: that in the seventh month, on the tenth day of the month, ye shall afflict your souls, and do no work at all, whether it be one of your own country, or a stranger that sojourneth among you: For on that day shall the priest make an atonement for you, to cleanse you, that ye may be clean from all your sins before the LORD.**
>
> —Leviticus 16:29–30

The rabbi once again ignores God plan for forgiveness of sin and how to become clean before Him. He used these verses in Isaiah to overrule the law of Moses and the requirements clearly outline in Leviticus 16.

Rabbis Singer on the blinded servant

In an attempt to discredit that the First Servant Song found in Isaiah 42 is about the Messiah, the rabbi mentioned the blinded servant of Isaiah 42. He then asked if Chaplain McTernan's Servant was blind. This was found in the second debate, part three which follows:

> Not as you say the Messiah is God's Servant. In fact the same Isaiah 42 you quote from, at the end of the chapter it says, who is blind but My servant. Is your Messiah blind? Now I know how it goes that there is two different servants in Isaiah 42 and three servants here, this is not true.

Chaplain McTernan's post debate response

The rabbi actually highlighted the two servants found in Isaiah. The first Servant, King Messiah, opens the eyes of blind. The second servant, Israel, is blinded because of sin. The distinction between the two servants is very apparent. The verses to show this follow:

God Righteous Servant, King Messiah:
> **Behold my servant, whom I uphold; mine elect, in whom my soul delighteth; I have put my spirit upon him: he shall bring forth judgment to the Gentiles. I the LORD have called thee in righteousness, and will hold thine hand, and will keep thee, and give thee for a covenant of the people, for a light of the Gentiles; To open the blind eyes, to bring out the prisoners from the prison, and them that sit in darkness out of the prison house.**

> —Isaiah 42:1,6–7

Israel God's Blinded Servant:
> **Who is blind, but my servant? or deaf, as my messenger that I sent? who is blind as he that is perfect, and blind as the Lord's servant? Seeing many things, but thou observest not;**

opening the ears, but he heareth not. . . . But this is a people robbed and spoiled; they are all of them snared in holes, and they are hid in prison houses: they are for a prey, and none delivereth; for a spoil, and none saith, Restore. . . . Who gave Jacob for a spoil, and Israel to the robbers? did not the LORD, he against whom we have sinned? for they would not walk in his ways, neither were they obedient unto his law.

—Isaiah 42:19–20,22,24

Isaiah 53 is about God's Righteous Servant, King Messiah and not about Israel the blinded servant.

Question One and Rabbi Singer on seeing God

During this question, the issue of man seeing God was raised. Chaplain McTernan used scriptures from Exodus 33 to show that Moses stood directly before the holy God of Israel and witnessed His form. Rabbi Singer's response follows:

You know the Bible says that God will not forsake the Jewish people, on the wings of eagles. Does that mean that God is a chicken? . . . This is called anthropomorphism. That God uses the language that we, man understands in order to communicate with us. You say we can't imagine, but God says in Numbers 23:19, that God is not a man, that He should lie. He is not mortal that He should repent. The exact same message is repeated, in 2 Samuel 15:29.

Chaplain McTernan's post debate response:

The Bible very explicitly shows that the holy God of Israel was present among the children of Israel. Exodus is a literal account of God interacting with His people and specifically Moses. It was not written as an allegory, but as a historical event. There were earthquakes and fire as God manifested Himself on the top of Mt. Sinai. The mass of people even heard His voice:

And Moses brought forth the people out of the camp to meet
with God . . . And mount Sinai was altogether on a smoke,
because the LORD descended upon it in fire: and the smoke
thereof ascended as the smoke of a furnace, and the whole
mount quaked greatly. And when the voice of the trumpet
sounded long, and waxed louder and louder, Moses spake,
and God answered him by a voice. And the LORD came down
upon mount Sinai, on the top of the mount. . . .

—Exodus 19:17–20

Later the Bible reveals that Moses and seventy–two others watched the
LORD from a distance. Moses described what they had witnessed:

Then went up Moses, and Aaron, Nadab, and Abihu, and seventy of the elders of Israel: And they saw the God of Israel:
and there was under his feet as it were a paved work of a sap-
phire stone, and as it were the body of heaven in his clear-
ness. And upon the nobles of the children of Israel he laid
not his hand: also they saw God, and did eat and drink.

—Exodus 24:9–11

God stated that Moses was different than all the other prophets. The
LORD would speak to the prophets in visions and dreams but not so
with Moses. He would speak directly to Moses and allow Moses to see
His similitude. This means a visible likeness.

My servant Moses is not so, who is faithful in all mine house.
With him will I speak mouth to mouth, even apparently, and
not in dark speeches; and the similitude of the LORD shall
he behold. . . .

— Numbers 12:7–8

God defines what it means to see Him: seeing God according to Exodus

34:30 means to look into His face. Moses looked at God's similitude, but he never looked directly into the face of God. According to the Bible, God has a form that we can recognize and at least seventy–three people during the Exodus saw God's form.

> **And he said, Thou canst not see my face: for there shall no man see me, and live.**
>
> —Exodus 33:20

The proof that Moses stood in God's direct presence is seen in Exodus 34. When Moses left God and came back to the people, they were afraid of him. Moses face radiantly glowed from being in God's presence, and the people were terrified of him. Moses had to put a veil over his face when speaking to the people to calm their fears.

> **And when Aaron and all the children of Israel saw Moses, behold, the skin of his face shone; and they were afraid to come nigh him. . . . And till Moses had done speaking with them, he put a veil on his face.**
>
> —Exodus 34:30,33

There is no doubt that Moses looked at the similitude of the LORD just as described in Exodus 33:17–23.

Chapter Five

Additional Teaching Material

Psalm 110:1 and 5
Adonai at the Right Hand of Jehovah

Psalm 110 was not a topic for the debate; however during the question and answer section, a significant amount of time was spent on this psalm. The following information adds to the concepts presented by Chaplain McTernan. This is only a partial teaching. For the full teaching, see Chaplain McTernan's book *Only Jesus of Nazareth Can Be the God of Israel's Righteous Servant.*

Psalm 110 was written by David. There is no doubt that he wrote it. There are fifty–eight psalms directly attributed to David, all beginning with "*A Psalm of David.*" No psalm starts with the heading "A Psalm about David" or "A Psalm to David." The heading for Psalm 110 is identical to the other fifty–seven; therefore, the subject of Psalm 110 is someone other than David. The first verse follows:

A Psalm of David. The LORD said unto my Lord, Sit thou at my right hand, until I make thine enemies thy footstool.

—Psalm 110:1

David starts with the first verse by stating, "*The LORD said unto my Lord.*" Since David was the king of Israel, His Lord has to be someone higher in authority than even him. This person needs the authority of a king, but on a higher level than David. Only one person fits this description, and that is Israel's eternal King. This is King Messiah who reigns forever over all the nations of the world. The prophet Daniel identifies Him as the "son of man." His origin is supernatural as He comes directly from Heaven to set up His eternal kingdom on earth. King Messiah is given dominion, glory, and a kingdom that will last forever. All of the nations of the earth will serve Him. King Messiah is David's Lord as shown in the following verses:

> **I saw in the night visions, and, behold, one like the Son of man came with the clouds of heaven, and came to the Ancient of days, and they brought him near before him. And there was given him dominion, and glory, and a kingdom, that all people, nations, and languages, should serve him: his dominion is an everlasting dominion, which shall not pass away, and his kingdom that which shall not be destroyed.**
>
> —Daniel 7:13–14

Great kings are chronicled in the Bible such as David and Solomon; however, none were ever placed in such a highly glorified position as described in Psalm 110. Not even Abraham or Moses were given the distinction of being placed at the right hand of the holy God of Israel. Rather, King Messiah will be at God's right hand of authority. He is the One whose throne is for all generations:

> **I have made a covenant with my chosen, I have sworn unto David my servant, Thy seed will I establish for ever, and build up thy throne to all generations.**
>
> —Psalm 89:3–4

The Hebrew uses two different words in Psalm 110:1 for Lord. The Hebrew word for David's Lord is "*adon*," referring to someone in authority, usually human authority. In addition to Lord, *adon* is also translated "master" or "owner." David recognizes that the person he is writing about has authority over him. The Hebrew word *adon* is a very strong indicator that this person is a human king. This King then becomes the central figure of Psalm 2.

The second word is LORD or Jehovah in English. The LORD is the holy God of Israel. David recognizes that his Lord is seated at the right hand of the LORD. The expression "*Sit thou at my right hand*" relates to power and authority. It means that whoever sits at the right hand of the LORD exercises all the authority of God. David's Lord has complete power and authority. This is the exact authority that King Messiah possesses.

David's identification of his Lord does not end in verse 1. Psalm 110:5 contains a tremendous revelation of Israel's King Messiah. This verse reveals a third Lord. This is the Hebrew word "*Adonai.*" *Adonai* is now at the right hand of the LORD in the same position as the "*Adon.*" The Hebrew word *Adonai* always refers to the God of Israel. This verse reveals that not only is David's Lord a human King, He also is the God of Israel! This is easily observed by examining the two verses placed together. Please carefully examine Psalm 110:1 and 5, which follow:

The LORD [Jehovah] said unto *my Lord* [*Adon*], Sit thou at *my right hand* [Jehovah], until I make thine enemies thy footstool.

—Psalm 110:1

The *Lord* [*Adonai*] at *thy right hand* [Jehovah] shall strike through kings in the day of his wrath.

—Psalm 110:5

Psalm 110:5 identifies the Lord on the right hand of the LORD in verse 1 as being the holy God of Israel. By looking at these two verses together, the conclusion is that *Adonai* is at the right hand of Jehovah! Therefore, in the context of both Psalm 110:1 and Psalm 110:5, the subject at the right hand of the LORD is both God [*Adonai*] and man [*Adon*].

The New Testament and Psalm 110: 1 and 5

The New Testament claims that the Messiah, Jesus of Nazareth, is seated at the right hand of the Father. The writer of the book of Acts claims that Psalm 110 is a direct reference to the Lord Jesus. Thus, He exercises all the authority of God:

> **This Jesus hath God raised up, whereof we all are witnesses. Therefore being by the right hand of God exalted, and having received of the Father the promise of the Holy Ghost, he hath shed forth this, which ye now see and hear. . . . For David is not ascended into the heavens: but he saith himself, The Lord said unto my Lord, Sit thou on my right hand, Until I make thy foes thy footstool.**
>
> —Acts 2:32,34

This New Testament concept of the Lord Jesus at the right hand of the LORD is therefore in perfect harmony with the Hebrew Scriptures. The New Testament expression for "*Adonai* at the right hand of Jehovah" is "the Son seated at the right hand of God." The verses to show this follow:

> **So then after the Lord had spoken unto them he was received up into heaven, and sat on the right hand of God.**
>
> —Mark 16:19

> **Who is gone into heaven, and is on the right hand of God; angels and authorities and powers being made subject unto him.**
>
> —1 Peter 3:22

> **If ye then be risen with Christ, seek those things which are above, where Christ sitteth on the right hand of God.**
>
> —Colossians 3:1

Genealogy of the Kings of Israel and the Need for the Virgin Birth

During the Question and Answer section of the debate, the topic of the Lord Jesus' genealogy was raised. This was not a topic of the debate, but just a question. Because of the limited time, it could only be dealt with superficially. Chaplain McTernan challenged Rabbi Singer to debate this topic, which he declined. Chaplain McTernan claimed Israel could not have a natural–born Messiah because the Old Testament revealed that the Messiah's genealogical line ended.

The following information adds to this concept. This is only a partial teaching. For the full teaching see Chaplain McTernan's book *Only Jesus of Nazareth Can Be Israel's King Messiah.*

The clear line of the Messiah starts with King David. God promised David that the Messiah would come through him. A direct descendant of David would sit on the throne as king in an everlasting kingdom. Although David would have many sons, God narrowed the messianic line through one of David's sons. The line would go through the son who would build the temple or as it is also called, the house of God.

David's son Solomon built the temple. It is his genealogy to follow for the messianic line. The only place in the Old Testament to find this genealogy is 1 Chronicles 3:1–24. Although Solomon had seven hundred wives and three hundred concubines, the Bible lists only one son for him, Rehoboam: "*And Solomon's son was **Rehoboam***" (1 Chron. 3:10).

The promise for David's seed to sit on the throne was conditional. The covenant was eternal to David but to his seed it was conditional. The kings failed the conditions of the covenant and God ended their line. God then moved to fulfill the eternal covenant with David by providing His own Son as the Messiah. The following scriptures show the covenant with David's seed through Solomon was conditional:

Now the days of David drew nigh that he should die; and he

**charged Solomon his son, saying, . . . And keep the charge
of the LORD thy God, to walk in his ways, to keep his statutes, and his commandments, and his judgments, and his
testimonies, as it is written in the law of Moses, that thou
mayest prosper in all that thou doest, and whithersoever
thou turnest thyself: That the LORD may continue his word
which he spake concerning me, saying,** *If thy children take
heed to their way, to walk before me in truth with all their
heart and with all their soul, there shall not fail thee (said he)
a man on the throne of Israel.*

—1 Kings 2:1–4

**And he said unto me, Solomon thy son, he shall build my
house and my courts: for I have chosen him to be my son,
and I will be his father. Moreover I will establish his kingdom for ever,** *if he be constant to do my commandments and
my judgments, as at this day.*

—1 Chronicles 28:6–7

*If thy children will keep my covenant and my testimony that I
shall teach them,* **their children shall also sit upon thy throne
for evermore.**

—Psalm 132:12

The kingly line from Solomon forward failed to keep the statutes and
commandments of the LORD. The first curse on the messianic line
came through King Hezekiah. Hezekiah was a good king and did that
which pleased God. God greatly blessed him, but Hezekiah made a huge
mistake that would drastically affect the future of the kings of Judah.
Babylon sent ambassadors to meet with Hezekiah. In a foolish moment, Hezekiah showed them all the great wealth of the kingdom.

After the ambassadors left, the prophet Isaiah came to Hezekiah
and asked him about showing the Babylonians the treasury. Isaiah

rebuked the king for being so proud to show the treasury to the pagans. Isaiah then pronounced a judgment on the king that all his descendants would be taken captive to Babylon and made eunuchs in the palace of the king of Babylon. Because of pride, Hezekiah showed all the wealth of the treasury. This would be the lure one hundred years later that would draw the Babylonians to destroy Jerusalem:

> **And Hezekiah was glad of them, and showed them the house of his precious things, the silver, and the gold, and the spices, and the precious ointment, and all the house of his armour, and all that was found in his treasures: there was nothing in his house, nor in all his dominion, that Hezekiah showed them not.... Then said Isaiah to Hezekiah, Hear the word of the LORD of hosts: Behold, the days come, that all that is in thine house, and that which thy fathers have laid up in store until this day, shall be carried to Babylon: nothing shall be left, saith the LORD. And of thy sons that shall issue from thee, which thou shalt beget, shall they take away; and they shall be eunuchs in the palace of the king of Babylon.**
>
> —Isaiah 39:2,5–7

The next king of Judah to bring judgment on the messianic line was Jeconiah. He is also called Coniah and Jehoiachin. All three names—Jeconiah, Coniah and Jehoiachin—refer to the same king of Judah. Jeconiah was an evil king and God was outraged with him. During Jeconiah's reign, God judged the kingly line with a curse. The curse was that no descendant of Jeconiah would sit as king of Israel. Jeconiah had children, but the prophet Jeremiah said to consider him childless. Jeconiah was removed as king and replaced with his uncle Zedekiah.

> **As I live, saith the LORD, though Coniah the son of Jehoiakim king of Judah were the signet upon my right hand, yet would I pluck thee thence; . . . O earth, earth, earth, hear the word**

**of the LORD. Thus saith the LORD, Write ye this man child-
less, a man that shall not prosper in his days: for no man of
his seed shall prosper, sitting upon the throne of David, and
ruling any more in Judah.**

—Jeremiah 22:24,29–30

This curse on king Jeconiah was made in the strongest possible language. The prophet said, "O earth, earth, earth, hear the word of the
Lord." The curse was initiated with a triple declaration of "earth, earth,
earth." This is the only time in the Bible that such a triple declaration
of a curse was made. This is unique in the entire Bible. There was no
remedy for this curse. It was not conditional. There is no indication
in the Scriptures that if Jeconiah repented the curse would be lifted.
This curse was final, and it was established forever. This curse is still
in effect. Any Jew today who is from the line of Jeconiah is forbidden
by this curse to sit as the king of Israel.

Zedekiah, the last king, rebelled against the king of Babylon and
was taken prisoner. All of the king's sons were killed by the Babylonians. The combination of the curse on the kingly line and the deaths
of all Zedekiah's sons ended the line from Solomon through Rehoboam.
From 586 B.C. when Nebuchadnezzar, king of Babylon, ended the
kingdom of Judah, there has not been a king to sit on the throne of
David. No son of David since that time has sat as the king of Israel.

**And the king of Babylon slew the sons of Zedekiah before his
eyes: he slew also all the princes of Judah in Riblah.**

—Jeremiah 52:10

The messianic line through Solomon thus was cut off and came to an
end. The line ended three ways. The sons of King Zedekiah were all
killed. A curse was placed on all the sons of King Jeconiah that they
could not sit on the throne of David as the king of Israel. The descendants of King Hezekiah were all made eunuchs in Babylon, and thus

they were unable to continue the messianic line.

The only descendants alive today from the messianic line are through Jeconiah. They would have the curse on them that they could never be the king of Israel. Israel cannot have a king because of the curse. Through the virgin birth of Jesus of Nazareth, God provided Israel with a king without the curse.